MHRA
STYLE BOOK

NOTES FOR
AUTHORS, EDITORS, AND
WRITERS OF DISSERTATIONS
(Third Edition)

Edited by

A. S. Maney and R. L. Smallwood
in consultation with
the Committee of the Association

LONDON
Modern Humanities Research Association
1981

First Edition published 1971
Reprinted (with amendments) 1973
Reprinted (with amendments) 1974
Reprinted 1976
Reprinted 1977
Second Edition 1978
Third Edition 1981
Reprinted 1984

Note

The purpose of this handbook is to assist authors and editors of academic publications, and those preparing dissertations, to achieve clarity and consistency in matters of style and presentation

The second edition was fully revised by the editors and a special sub-committee of the MHRA under the chairmanship of Professor Glanville Price. This third edition has amplified the guidance given on the citation of manuscripts and has introduced a new sub-section on the citation of references by the Author–Date System.

ISBN 0 900547 79 0

Printed by W. S. Maney & Son Ltd, Leeds, England

Contents

1   PREPARING THE TYPESCRIPT   PAGE

     (a)   General   1

     (b)   Headings   1

     (c)   Numbering of Pages   1

     (d)   Copies   2

     (e)   Notes   2

     (f)   Subdivisions   2

     (g)   Corrections, Insertions, and Comments . .   2

     (h)   Checking   3

     (i)   Foreign Languages   3

     (j)   Hyphens   4

     (k)   Type Faces   4

     (l)   Illustrations   5

     (m)   Running Headings   6

     (n)   Cross-References   6

     (o)   Order of Parts of a Book   6

2   SPELLING

     (a)   Preferred Spellings   8

     (b)   Accents   8

     (c)   Hyphens   8

     (d)   Quotations   9

     (e)   The Possessive   10

     (f)   Place-Names   10

3   ABBREVIATIONS

     (a)   General   11

     (b)   Of Titles   11

     (c)   In Footnotes and Endnotes   11

     (d)   Use of Full Stop   12

     (e)   Omissions   12

4 PUNCTUATION PAG
  (a) Commas I
  (b) Dashes I
  (c) Parentheses and Brackets I
  (d) Punctuation in Headings I
  (e) Punctuation with Italics I
  (f) Quotation Marks I
  (g) Exclamation Marks I
  (h) Ellipsis I

5 CAPITALIZATION
  (a) General I
  (b) Titles and Dignities I
  (c) Literary Movements and Periods . . . I
  (d) Titles of Books and Other Writings . . . I
  (e) Hyphenated Compounds in Titles and Headings . I
  (f) Accented Capitals I

6 ITALICS
  (a) General I
  (b) Foreign Words and Quotations I
  (c) Titles of Books and Other Writings . . . 2

7 DATES, NUMBERS, AND CURRENCY
  (a) Dates 2
  (b) Numbers 2
  (c) Roman Numerals 2
  (d) Currency 2

8 QUOTATIONS AND QUOTATION MARKS
  (a) General 2
  (b) In Foreign Languages 2
  (c) Short Quotations 2

PAGE

(d) Long Quotations 25
(e) Omissions 27
(f) Copyright 27

9 FOOTNOTES
(a) General 29
(b) Methods of Limiting Footnotes 29
(c) Position and Numbering 30

10 REFERENCES
(a) General 31
(b) Forms of Reference 32
    (i) Books 32
    (ii) Articles in Books 35
    (iii) Articles in Journals 36
    (iv) Articles in Newspapers 37
    (v) Dissertations and Theses 37
    (vi) Plays and Long Poems 37
    (vii) The Bible 38
    (viii) Manuscripts 38
(c) Later References 39
(d) Citation by the Author–Date System . . . 40
(e) Cross-References 42
(f) Bibliographies 42

11 PRESENTATION OF THESES AND DISSERTATIONS
(a) General 43
(b) The Length of the Thesis 43
(c) Parts of the Thesis 43
    (i) Title-Page 43
    (ii) Summary or Synopsis 44
    (iii) Table of Contents and List of Illustrations . 44
    (iv) Preface, Acknowledgements, Declaration . 45
    (v) List of Abbreviations 45
    (vi) Text 45

PAGE

      (vii) Notes 45
   (viii) Appendices 46
     (ix) Bibliography 46
      (x) Index 46
(d) Preparation of the Final Typescript . . . 47
      (i) General 47
     (ii) Paper, Type Face, and Margins . . . 47
   (iii) Spacing 47
   (iv) Pagination 48
    (v) Headings and Subheadings . . . 48
   (vi) Checking and Correction 48
  (vii) Cross-References 48
 (viii) Illustrations 49
   (ix) Number of Copies 49
(e) Binding 49
(f) Permission to Consult and Copy 50
(g) Further Reading 50

12 GLOSSARY 51

13 USEFUL WORKS OF REFERENCE 58

14 PROOF CORRECTION 59

15 INDEX 70

I

Preparing the Typescript

This section is concerned with the preparation of typescript for the press. For requirements relating specifically to the preparation of theses and dissertations, see Section 11 below.

(a) GENERAL

Copy should be typed on one side only of good white paper, preferably A4. The lines should be double-spaced and the same type size and face should be used throughout. Ample margins should be left all round and the top quarter of the first page left clear. A good ribbon should be used, and the typing should be reasonably consistent in the length of line and the number of lines per page. The first line of each paragraph (except the first paragraph of a chapter) should be indented four spaces and the space between paragraphs should be the normal double-spacing.

(b) HEADINGS

Do not type headings or subheadings entirely in capitals and do not underline them, since either method may conflict with the style which the editor wishes the printer to follow. No punctuation marks should be used after headings and subheadings.

(c) NUMBERING OF PAGES

The pages should be numbered consecutively in the top right-hand corner and the total number of pages in the typescript should be indicated at the head of the first page. The author's name and address should be typed in the top left-hand corner of the first page and it is advisable for the author of an article to type his surname before the number on each page. If any pages are removed or added during revision all the pages should be renumbered in sequence throughout. Do not staple the leaves of the typescript together; a removable paper-clip is preferable.

(d) COPIES

The top copy should always be sent to the editor or printer. A carbon copy carefully corrected against the top copy, or, perhaps better, a xerox print of the corrected top copy, should be kept by the author.

(e) NOTES

Whether they are to be printed as footnotes, or at the end of an article, chapter, or book, notes should be typed with double spacing throughout and should begin on a new sheet of paper at the end of the typescript. They should be numbered consecutively throughout an article or chapter, but not throughout a whole book, and each section should be headed 'Notes to Chapter . . .'. The notes will normally be set by the printer in type smaller than that used for the text; they are therefore set separately, and should be kept separate in the typescript. Care should be taken to check that the reference numbers in the text are in their correct places and that they agree with the numbers of the corresponding notes. The reference numbers in the text should be typed above the line without punctuation (at the ends of sentences if possible) and the editor should encircle these numbers in ink as he checks them; this is a considerable help to the printer.

(f) SUBDIVISIONS

Major subdivisions within an article or chapter, if required, should be marked by increased spacing and the author should insert the words 'extra space' and encircle them. In a work with numbered subdivisions a convenient order for designating these would be: capital roman numerals; capital letters; arabic numerals; lower-case letters; small roman numerals. Where there are fewer categories a selection may be made.

(g) CORRECTIONS, INSERTIONS, AND COMMENTS

If corrections or insertions are brief, type or write them legibly above the line involved. Proof-correcting conventions need not be followed at this stage. The margins should be left clear for editorial use. If a correction or an addition is of considerable length, type it on a separate *full-sized* sheet and mark it, and the position where it is to be inserted, clearly (for example, 'Insert A, page 5'). Pages with extensive alteration should be retyped; the reverse of the page should never be used. Comments or questions for the editor may be noted in pencil in the margin so that they may be erased later. Special comments to be brought to the attention of the printer should be written near the top of the page, encircled, and preceded by the word 'PRINTER' (in capitals).

(h) CHECKING

Typescripts should be carefully checked before they are forwarded to the editor or printer. In particular, all quotations must be checked against the originals; this checking must never be left to the proof stage. Though the printer does not charge for correcting his own errors, he is entitled to charge for author's corrections, and the charges for such corrections can be high. An editor has the right to expect that an author's typescript is final and authors should not be surprised to be informed that no author's corrections can be permitted on the proof or, if they are permitted, that the author must bear the cost.

(i) FOREIGN LANGUAGES

In languages other than English, accents may present problems to the printer and care should be taken with them. Accents which are not available on the typewriter should be inserted clearly in ink. Ligatures should also be indicated by hand: 'o͡e' for 'œ', etc. Other characters not available on the typewriter, for example the German double s (β), may have to be similarly indicated.

If an author's work makes use of any characters which are not in normal use in Western European languages, he should draw attention to this fact by a note attached to his typescript. It would be helpful to list the characters in question and indicate which of these he has used frequently and which are used only once or twice. This will enable the printer to establish, at an early stage, which of these characters he can make available on his typesetting machine. He may then make arrangements for obtaining and, if necessary, inserting by hand, those characters which he cannot so accommodate.

Authors who wish to make substantial use of non-roman characters or transliteration should conform with the requirements of the editor or publisher for whom their work is intended. The following publications contain much useful information on copy-preparation and typesetting for foreign languages, both roman and non-roman:

> Horace Hart, *Hart's Rules for Compositors and Readers at the University Press, Oxford*, thirty-eighth edition (Oxford, 1978), pp. 88–134
>
> University of Chicago Press, *A Manual of Style*, twelfth edition (Chicago, 1970), pp. 209–33

(j) HYPHENS

If a line ends with a hyphen it may not be clear to the printer, particularly if the passage is in a foreign language, whether he is to set the word as a hyphenated compound or as one word. When a broken word is not to be hyphenated this should be indicated in the margin by curved lines (⌒) to show that the parts of the word are to be joined. For words not so marked the printer will normally follow copy and print the hyphen. This problem may be avoided if the typist is instructed never to allow a break in a foreign word at the end of a line but to carry over the whole word to the next line. (See also Section 2 (c) below.)

(k) TYPE FACES

The following alphabets may be available on a composing (typesetting) machine:

CAPITALS	SMALL CAPITALS	lower case
ITALIC CAPITALS		*italic lower case*
BOLD CAPITALS		**bold lower case**

These should be indicated on the typescript in the following manner: *italics* by single underlining of the relevant words or letters; SMALL CAPITALS by two lines under small letters; LARGE CAPITALS by typing capitals or by three lines under small letters; *ITALIC LARGE CAPITALS* by one line under ordinary capitals or by four lines under small letters; **bold type** by a wavy underline.

Authors should note, however, that some composing machines cannot accommodate all the seven alphabets specified above. Such limitations apply particularly to 'strike-on' machines and certain photosetters. Even when a machine is to be used which offers a wide range of characters it may not be possible to use all seven founts if many accented or unusual characters are required. In such circumstances it is usual to dispense with the bold type or the small capitals in order to make space available for the special characters which a particular work requires.

Passages such as long quotations which are to be set in a smaller type than the text, or with reduced leading, or indented, should be typed to the normal measure and should be marked off by extra space above and below the quoted passage. A vertical line should be drawn in the margin against the quoted passage and the editor (not the author) will indicate the precise style of printing to be used for such marked passages.

(1) ILLUSTRATIONS

For line illustrations, provide a clear original in black ink on white paper or board; for halftone illustrations, a glossy black-and-white bromide print. Indicate clearly on the reverse of each drawing or photograph the figure or plate number in the article or book and the required size for the block. (Be careful to write very lightly on the reverse of photographs or they may be spoiled.) Some reduction may improve definition, but excessive reduction may cause detail, such as fine lines or close shading, to be lost. Normally the original ought not to be more than four times larger, nor should it be appreciably smaller, than the required block. A decision concerning the size of the block should take account of the area occupied by the type on a page of the relevant journal or book, and the size of the block should fit approximately into this pattern. If part of the illustration is to be omitted, indicate lightly on the reverse the portion which is to be masked off.

If any lettering on a drawing needs to be re-drawn, or replaced by printer's type, this should be noted. Indicate the approximate required position, relative to the text, for each illustration, but bear in mind that, for technical reasons, it may not be possible to place the illustration exactly.

Captions for illustrations should be typed on a separate sheet and attached to the typescript. Illustrations should be numbered in sequence throughout an article or book, plates in roman numerals, figures in arabic. Where appropriate, the scale of an illustration in relation to the original should be indicated. Acknowledgement of permission to reproduce the illustration, where appropriate, should be included below the caption or in the preliminary list of illustrations.

Original illustrations should be very carefully packed to avoid damage: a strong piece of cardboard in the envelope is advisable. Do not use paper-clips to hold photographs together.

(m) RUNNING HEADINGS

Shortened headings may be required at the heads of pages after the first page of the article or chapter. It will assist the editor and printer if suitable abbreviated versions of the relevant titles are suggested.

(n) CROSS-REFERENCES

Cross-references within an article or book should be indicated by typed zeros, encircled in ink:

See above (or below) p. (ooo) note (o.)

The typescript page number referred to should be pencilled in the margin and such cross-references should be carefully checked on the proofs.

(o) ORDER OF PARTS OF A BOOK

Before despatch to the printer the typescript of a book should be arranged in the following order (though few books will include all the items listed below):

Half-title (the full title of the book, and the title of the series and the volume number in that series, if applicable; the name of the author does not normally appear; the verso of this page is usually left blank when the book is printed)

Title-page

Bibliographical details (name and address of publisher and printer, copyright, International Standard Book Number (ISBN), etc.)

Dedication or epigraph (the verso is left blank)

Contents list

List of illustrations (plates, figures, maps, and tables, in that order)

Foreword (by someone other than the author)

Author's preface

Acknowledgements (if not included in the author's preface)

List of abbreviations and/or glossary if these are necessary to an understanding of the text; otherwise they may be placed towards the end of the book, before the bibliography

Introduction (unless this constitutes the first chapter of the text)

Text

Appendix or appendices

Notes and references (for the whole typescript)

Bibliography

Index

If there is a frontispiece illustration it should face the title-page. The copyright should be indicated thus: international copyright symbol; name of holder of copyright; year of first publication. The name of the country where the book was printed must appear and may conveniently be combined with the printer's imprint. All principal items should, when the book is printed, begin on a right-hand page. The preliminary pages, comprising all items before the main text, are usually numbered in lower-case roman numerals; though these numbers are not printed on certain pages (half-title, title, etc.), they are counted in the sequence. Arabic numbering usually begins on the first page of the text. However, since the page numbers cannot be added by the printer until the page proofs are prepared, *all* the pages of the typescript should be numbered in one (arabic) sequence throughout (see Section 1 (c) above).

2

Spelling

(a) PREFERRED SPELLINGS

British spelling (as given in the *Oxford English Dictionary* and its derivatives) should be used. For verbs ending in 'ize' or 'ise', the 'ize' form is preferred. Some verbs, however, with their compounds and derivatives, must have the 'ise' spelling, e.g.:

advertise	comprise	devise	franchise	revise
advise	compromise	enterprise	improvise	supervise
apprise	demise	excise	incise	surmise
chastise	despise	exercise	premise	surprise

For other alternative spellings, the form given in the *Oxford Dictionary for Writers and Editors* (Oxford, 1981) should be used.

(b) ACCENTS

The normal practice for foreign words which have passed into regular English usage is for accents to be dropped: thus accents are no longer used on 'denouement', 'levee', 'role', etc. But for reasons of pronunciation 'café', 'cliché', etc. retain their accents. (See also Section 5 (e) below, and the *Oxford Dictionary for Writers and Editors*.)

(c) HYPHENS

Hyphens should not be used loosely but only where they serve a definite purpose. They are normally needed to indicate that two or more words are to be read together as a single word with its own meaning. If the two (or more) parts of a phrase are separately and equally stressed they usually remain as separate words unhyphenated. Thus:

coat of arms	free will
common sense	well known
fifteenth century	White Paper

If such phrases are used attributively they are normally hyphenated:

common-sense argument	free-will offering
fifteenth-century manuscript	well-known fact

Hyphens should be used where necessary to avoid ambiguity:

two year-old dogs	two-year-old dogs
deep blue lake	deep-blue lake
recover	re-cover

and to avoid an awkward collocation of letters:

looking-glass	re-enter

The tendency is for a combination of words which constitute a single concept to come into use as a hyphenated compound but for the hyphen to be dropped when the compound is commonly used, provided that the resultant close (or solid) compound is not awkward to read. Thus we have:

anybody	dustman	reprint
aerofoil	horsepower	screenplay
bookshelf	motorway	subscript
battlefield	paperback	twofold

If a compound is in frequent use and is pronounced as one word with a single stress it is usually correct to write it as one word without a hyphen. It must be admitted that there is much variety in the use of hyphens and it is almost impossible to formulate comprehensive rules in this respect, but an author should be consistent. (See also Section 1 (j) above.)

(d) QUOTATIONS

The spelling of quotations is always that of the book or edition referred to. But in quotations from early printed books the forms of the letters 'i' and 'j', 'u' and 'v', the long 's', the ampersand (&), the nunnation mark (tilde), superior letters in contractions, and other abbreviations are normalized to modern usage unless there are good reasons to the contrary, as, for example, in bibliographical descriptions.

(e) THE POSSESSIVE

Form the possessive of proper names ending in *s* or another sibilant by adding an apostrophe and *s*:

Keats's poems, Marx's theories

Consistency is desirable and the rule applies regardless of the number of syllables; cacophony can be avoided by periphrasis:

Lawrence's novels, Alvarez's criticism, the plays of Euripides

French names ending in an unpronounced *s* or *x* will also need an apostrophe and a pronounced *s* to indicate the possessive in English:

Rabelais's comedy, Camus's novels, Descartes's works, Malraux's style

(f) PLACE-NAMES

Where there is a normal English form for foreign place-names (Munich, Naples, Venice, Lisbon, Vienna, etc.), it should be used in preference to the native form unless there are good reasons to the contrary. Rare or obsolete English forms (Leipsic, Francfort, etc.) are, however, best avoided. (On place-names in references to the publication of books, see Sections 10 (b) (i) and 10 (f) below.)

3
Abbreviations

(a) GENERAL

Since abbreviations increase the possibility of confusion and misunderstanding, they should be used with caution. When writing for a particular publication, use only those abbreviations which are likely to be familiar to its readers. Never begin a sentence with an abbreviation, and avoid abbreviations as far as possible in passages of continuous prose. For example:

> The author's comments on page 47, line 20, seem particularly apt.

Here the words 'page' and 'line', normally abbreviated in references, are given in full to prevent a jerky effect in reading. Extensively used abbreviations should be clearly listed at the beginning of a book or in an early footnote to an article; the first use of an abbreviation should refer the reader to this list.

(b) OF TITLES

Avoid inelegant or confusing abbreviations of the titles of works of literature, especially in continuous prose. It is usually preferable to write *A la recherche du temps perdu*, not *RTP*; *All's Well that Ends Well*, not *All's Well*. However, in repeated references to a work some abbreviation of long titles may be appropriate. (But see below, Section 9 (b), on the desirability of avoiding repeated footnote references to the same text.)

(c) IN FOOTNOTES AND ENDNOTES

If possible, do not begin a note with an abbreviation which is normally printed in lower-case characters ('e.g.', 'i.e.', 'pp.'). If this cannot be avoided, the initial letters of footnotes should remain in lower case:

[21] pp. 127–39 *not* [21] Pp. 127–39

(d)   USE OF FULL STOP

A contracted form of a word, ending with the same letter as the full form, including plurals, is not followed by a full stop:

Mr   Dr   Mrs   vols   St

Other abbreviations take the full stop:

Esq.   vol.   p.   pp.   a.m.   M. (Monsieur)

Where the initial letters of each word of the title of a journal are used as an abbreviated title, full stops are omitted:

MLR   PMLA   TLS

The full stop is also omitted after the abbreviation for 'manuscript' in both singular and plural:

MS   MSS

It is also preferable to omit full stops after initial capitals used as abbreviations for well-known institutions and organized bodies:

BM   BL   PRO   MHRA   UNESCO

(e)   OMISSIONS

Some words are abbreviated by omitting the first part of the word. If such abbreviations are in common use, no apostrophe is needed:

bus *not* 'bus
phone *not* 'phone
the twenties (i.e. 1920s) *not* 'twenties

4

Punctuation

(a) COMMAS

In enumeration of three or more items, the words 'and' and 'or' should be preceded by a comma to avoid ambiguity:

He wrote plays, novels, and short stories.
But: He wrote plays, novels and short stories, and a treatise on prosody.

You may travel by car, bus, or train.
But: You may travel by car, bus or tram, or bicycle.

(b) DASHES

The printer has at his disposal both short and long dashes and neither of these symbols is available on the typewriter. The short dash ('en rule') is used to indicate a span or a differentiation and may usually be considered as a substitute for 'and' or 'to'. It is represented in typescript by a double hyphen, unspaced:

the England–Australia test match
the London–Leeds motorway
the 1939–45 war
pp. 81–101

Long dashes ('em rules') are used in pairs to enclose parenthetical statements, or singly to denote a break in a sentence:

Some people — an ever increasing number — deplore this.
Family and fortune, health and happiness — all were gone.

The long dash is represented in typescript by a double hyphen preceded and followed by a space.

Long dashes should be used sparingly; commas, colons, or parentheses are often more appropriate. Other punctuation marks should not normally be used before or after a dash.

A very long dash (——), known to printers as a 2-em dash, is used to indicate 'ditto' in bibliographies and similar lists. It may be represented in typescript by a treble hyphen.

(c) PARENTHESES AND BRACKETS

Parentheses ( ) are used for parenthetical statements and references within a text. When a passage within parentheses falls at the end of a sentence of which it is only a part, the final full stop is placed outside the closing parenthesis:

> This was well reviewed at the time (for instance in *TLS*, 9 July 1971, p. 817).

When a complete sentence is within parentheses, the final full stop should be inside the closing parenthesis. If one parenthetical statement lies within another, use a further pair of parentheses:

> (His presidential address (1967) made this point clearly.)

This is quite unambiguous and there is no need to adopt the algebraic practice of using square brackets within parentheses.

Square brackets [ ] should be used for the enclosure of phrases or words which have been added to the original text or for editorial and similar comments:

> He adds that 'the lady [Mrs Jervis] had suffered great misfortunes'.
> I do not think they should have . . . [conclusion illegible].
> He swore to tell the truth, the old [*sic*] truth, and nothing but the truth.

Square brackets should also be used to enclose phonetic transcriptions. (On the use of square brackets in references to the publication of books, see Section 10 (b) (i) below.)

(d) PUNCTUATION IN HEADINGS

Punctuation marks (other than question or exclamation marks) should be omitted at the end of headings and sub-headings. Punctuation marks should also be omitted after items in lists which are in tabular form (except, of course, full stops used to mark abbreviations).

(e) PUNCTUATION WITH ITALICS

There are italic forms of most marks of punctuation except the full stop. The type style (roman or italics) of the main part of any sentence will govern the style of the punctuation marks within or concluding it. If the main part of a sentence is in roman but an italic word within it immediately precedes a mark of punctuation, that mark will normally be in roman. But if the punctuation mark occurs within a phrase or title which is entirely in italics, or if the punctuation mark belongs to the phrase in italics rather than to the sentence as a whole, the punctuation mark will be in italics:

Where is a storm more brilliantly portrayed than in Conrad's *Typhoon?*

In *Edmund Ironside; or, War Hath Made All Friends*, a play that survives in manuscript, we see this technique in operation.

Kingsley followed this with *Westward Ho!*, perhaps his best-known novel.

Who wrote *Who's Afraid of Virginia Woolf??*

(f) QUOTATION MARKS

See Section 8 below. (For the use of quotation marks with the titles of poems, essays, etc., see Section 6 (c) below.)

(g) EXCLAMATION MARKS

These should be used sparingly.

(h) ELLIPSIS

Type three full stops spaced on either side to indicate that words have been omitted:

For a tomb they have an altar . . . and for pity, praise.

If the ellipsis indicates the omission of the end of a sentence, it should be followed by an additional full stop (but see also Section 8 (e)). It should be preceded by a full stop if it follows a completed sentence.

5
Capitalization

(a) GENERAL

Initial capitals should be used with restraint; in doubtful instances it is usually best not to capitalize. Certain adjectives deriving from nouns taking initial capitals are not normally capitalized. For example:

Bible—biblical; Satan—satanic; Latin—latinate; Alps—alpine

Capitals must, however, be used for the initial letters of sentences, and for the names of places, persons, months, days, and nationalities. They are also to be used for the titles of laws, plans, wars, treaties, legal cases, and for specific institutions and other organized bodies (the Modern Humanities Research Association, the Poetry Book Club). Capitals are used also for unique events and periods (the Flood, the Last Judgement, the French Revolution, the Peasants' Revolt, the Iron Age), and for the parts of books when referred to specifically (Chapter 9, Appendix A, Figure 8, Plate VII). Do not use initial capitals for the seasons of the year or for the points of the compass except when the latter are abbreviated or used to indicate a specific place or area, for example, 'the North', indicating the northern region of England.

(b) TITLES AND DIGNITIES

Capitals are used for titles and dignities when these appear in full or immediately preceding a personal name, or when they are used specifically:

The Archbishop of Canterbury and the Bishop of Worcester were present, but Bishop Wilberforce was not.

But:

Several archbishops and bishops were present.

When, after a first full reference, or with such a reference understood, a title is used incompletely but still with specific application to an individual, the capital is retained:

The Archbishop spoke first.

A word or phrase used as a substitute for, or an extension of, a personal name also takes initial capitals:

the Iron Duke   Alfred the Great   the Dark Lady of the Sonnets

(c) LITERARY MOVEMENTS AND PERIODS

Capitals must be used for nouns and adjectives denoting cultural, philosophical, literary, and artistic movements and periods when these are derived from proper nouns:

Cartesian   Erastian   Stoic

They should also be used to refer to particular artistic and cultural movements when the use of a lower-case initial might cause confusion with the same word in a more general sense:

a poet of the Romantic school
a novel with a straightforwardly romantic plot

Other words may similarly require capitalization when they are used to refer to specific cultural movements ('Classical', 'Symbolist', 'Existentialist', 'neo-Platonic', 'neo-Classical', 'post-Romantic', etc.) or to specific historical periods ('the Renaissance', 'the Reformation', 'the Enlightenment', etc.).

(d) TITLES OF BOOKS AND OTHER WRITINGS

In most modern European languages except English and French, and in Latin and transliterated Slavonic languages, capitalization in the titles of books, essays, poems, etc. follows the rules of capitalization in normal prose. That is: the first word and all proper nouns (in German all nouns) take an initial capital, and all other words take a lower-case initial:

La vida es sueño   Il seme sotto la neve
Autorenlexikon der deutschen Gegenwartsliteratur

In English titles the initial letters of the first word and of all subsequent principal words (excluding articles, prepositions, conjunctions, and possessive adjectives) are capitalized:

> *All's Well that Ends Well*, *A Tale of Two Cities*, 'Mariana in the Moated Grange', 'Of Death'

English works with foreign titles are normally capitalized according to the English convention rather than that of the language of the title:

> *Religio Medici*,   *Apologia pro Vita Sua*,   'La Figlia che Piange'

In French titles it is normally only the initial letters of the first word and of proper nouns which are capitalized. But if the first word is an article, the following noun and any preceding adjectives also take an initial capital:

> *Le Père Goriot*, *A la recherche du temps perdu*, *Le Médecin malgré lui*, 'Colloque sentimental',   *Les Petits Riens*,   *Histoire de la peinture en Italie*

However, for reasons of logic, analogy, etc., capitals are sometimes used elsewhere:

> *Le Corbeau et le Renard*, *Le Rouge et le Noir*

(e) HYPHENATED COMPOUNDS IN TITLES AND HEADINGS

Capitalize the first part of the compound and capitalize the second part if it is a noun, or a proper adjective, or if it is equal in importance to the first part:

> Non-Christian   Anglo-Jewish Literature
> Seventeenth-Century Music   Vice-Chairman

The second part does not take a capital if it merely modifies the first part or if both parts are essentially one word:

> Democracy Re-established

(f) ACCENTED CAPITALS

Accents should be retained on all capitals in foreign languages if they would be used with the equivalent lower-case letters. The single exception to this is the French word *à* which always drops the *grave* accent when capitalized.

6

Italics

(a) GENERAL

Be sparing in the use of italics for rhetorical emphasis. Any word or phrase individually discussed should, however, be in italics, and any interpretation of it in single quotation marks:

He glosses *pale* as 'fenced land, park'.

(b) FOREIGN WORDS AND QUOTATIONS

Single words or short phrases in foreign languages not used as direct quotations from another writer should be in italics. Direct, acknowledged, or more substantial quotations should be in roman type (in small print or within single quotation marks). Avoid the formerly common practice of using italics if such quotations are in Latin or medieval German; quotations in these languages are treated in the same way as those in other languages. (On the setting of quotations see Section 8 below.)

Foreign words and phrases which have passed into regular English usage should not be italicized, though the decision between italic and roman type may sometimes be a fine one. In doubtful instances it is usually best to use roman. The following are examples of words which are no longer italicized:

cliché	ennui	milieu	role
debris	genre	par excellence	salon
denouement	leitmotif	per cent	status quo
dilettante	lemma	résumé	vice versa

(See also Section 2 (b) above, and the *Oxford Dictionary for Writers and Editors*.) Certain Latin words and abbreviations which are in common English usage are also no longer italicized. For example:

cf., e.g., etc., ibid., i.e., op. cit., passim

An exception is made of the Latin *sic*, frequently used within quotations (see Section 4 (c) above) and therefore conveniently differentiated by the use of italic. (See also Sections 10 (a) and 10 (c) below on the use of such abbreviations.)

(c) TITLES OF BOOKS AND OTHER WRITINGS

Italics are used for the titles of all works individually published under their own titles: books, journals, plays, longer poems, pamphlets, and any other entire published works (with certain exceptions such as the Bible and books of the Bible). But the titles of chapters in books or of articles in journals should be in roman type enclosed within single quotation marks; the titles of poems or essays which form part of a larger volume or other whole, or the first lines of poems used as titles, should also be given in roman type in single quotation marks:

> Théophile Gautier's 'L'Art'; Keats's 'Ode on a Grecian Urn'; Shelley's 'Music, When Soft Voices Die'; Bacon's 'Of Superstition'

The titles of collections of manuscripts should be given in roman type without quotation marks (see Section 10 (b) (viii) below). The titles of unpublished books and articles should be given in roman type within single quotation marks.

Titles of other works which appear within an italicized title should be printed in italics and enclosed in single quotation marks:

> *An Approach to 'Hamlet'*

In the citation of legal cases the names of the contending parties are given in italics, but the intervening 'v.' (for 'versus') is in roman: '*Bardell* v. *Pickwick*'.

7

Dates, Numbers, and Currency

(a) DATES

Dates should be given in the form '23 April 1564'. The name of the month should always appear in full between the day (23, *not* 23rd) and the year. No internal punctuation should be used. If it is necessary to refer to a date in both Old and New Styles the form '11/22 July 1705' should be used. For dates dependent upon the time of beginning the new year the form '21 January 1564/5' should be used. When referring to a period of time use the form 'from 1826 to 1850' (*not* 'from 1826–50'), 'from January to March 1970' (*not* 'from January–March 1970'). In citations of the era, 'B.C.' follows the year and 'A.D.' precedes it, and small capitals are used:

54 B.C.   A.D. 367

In references to decades an *s* without an apostrophe should be used:

the 1920s (*not* the 1920's)

In references to centuries the ordinal should be spelled out:

the sixteenth century (*not* the 16th century)

In giving approximate dates *circa* should be abbreviated as *c.*:

c. 1490   *c.* 300 B.C.

(b) NUMBERS

Numbers up to one hundred, including ordinals, when they form part of a narrative and are not statistical, should be written in words. Volume, part, chapter, and page numbers may be regarded as statistical and numerals should be used for these. Numerals are also used for years, including those below one hundred (see Section 7 (a) above). But time, numbers at the beginning of sentences, and approximate numbers, should be expressed in words:

He arrived at six forty-five.
Two hundred and forty-seven pages were written.
The fire destroyed about five thousand books.

In expressing inclusive numbers falling within the same hundred, the last two figures should be given:

13–15, 20–27, 44–47, 363–67, 1933–39

Note that a short dash, best represented in typescript by a double hyphen, is used, without spacing, between each pair of numbers.

Numbers which express dates before the Christian era should be stated in full since the shorter form could be misleading:

Nebuchadnezzar (1792–1750 B.C.)
not Nebuchadnezzar (1792–50 B.C.)

(c) ROMAN NUMERALS

The use of roman numerals should be confined to a few specific purposes:

(i)   large capitals for the ordinals of monarchs (Edward VII), and for major subdivisions within a text;

(ii)   small capitals for volume numbers of books (journals take arabic numerals), also for the acts of plays, for 'books' or other major subdivisions of long poems, novels, etc., and for certain documents;

(iii) lower case for the preliminary pages of a book or journal, where these are numbered separately, and for minor subdivisions within a text.

(d) CURRENCY

Words should be used to express simple sums of money occurring in normal prose:

The manuscript was sold for eight shillings in 1865.
The reprint costs eighty pence.
The fee was three hundred francs.

Sums of money which are cumbrous to express in words, or sums occurring in statistical tables etc., may be written in figures. British currency before 1971 should be shown in the following form:

The manuscript was sold for £197 12s. 6d. in 1965.

British decimal currency should be expressed in pounds and pence separated by a full stop on the line, not by a comma:

£12.65 *not* £12,65 or £12.65p

Sums below one pound should be shown thus (without a full stop after 'p'):

84p   6p   ½p

Abbreviations may be used for the more familiar foreign currencies where it is not appropriate to express sums in words. The following abbreviations precede the figures (without a full stop):

U.S.A. $ Netherlands   fl   West Germany   DM

Other abbreviations follow the figures and take full stops:

Austria   Sch.
Denmark ⎫
Norway ⎬ Kr. (D.Kr., N.Kr., S.Kr. if ambiguity is possible)
Sweden ⎭
France   F.
Switzerland Sw.F. (F. if no ambiguity is possible)

The names of other currencies should be written out in full, at least on the first occurrence.

8

Quotations and Quotation Marks

(a) GENERAL

Avoid the practice of using quotation marks as an oblique excuse for a loose, slang, or imprecise (and possibly inaccurate) word or phrase. Quotation marks should normally be reserved to indicate direct quotation from other writers.

In quoted passages follow the original for spelling, capitalization, italics, and punctuation (but see Section 2 (d) above and Section 8 (c) below).

(b) IN FOREIGN LANGUAGES

Quotations in foreign languages (including Latin and medieval German) are treated in the same way as those in English (see Section 6 (b) above). Unless there are special reasons to the contrary, the forms of quotation marks in foreign languages (« » „„." etc.) should be normalized to English usage.

(c) SHORT QUOTATIONS

Short quotations (not more than about sixty words of prose or two complete lines of verse) should be enclosed in single quotation marks and run on with the main text. If, however, there are several such short quotations coming close together and being compared or contrasted, or otherwise set out as examples, it may be appropriate to treat them in the same way as longer quotations (see Section 8 (d) below). If not more than two complete lines of verse are quoted but the quotation includes a line division, this should be marked with an upright stroke (|). For a quotation within a quotation, double quotation marks should be used:

He goes on to quote 'Then murmured Arthur "Place me in the barge" '

If a short quotation is used within a sentence, the final full stop should be outside the closing quotation mark; it may also be appropriate to alter an initial capital in such a quotation to lower case:

Do not be afraid of what Stevenson calls 'a little judicious levity'.

Carton's assertion that 'it is a far, far better thing that I do, than I have ever done' has become almost proverbial.

This rule applies even when a quotation ends with a full stop in the original, and when a quotation forms a complete sentence in the original but, as quoted, is integrated within a sentence of introduction or comment:

Dr Johnson believes that the play is 'one of the most amusing of our author's performances'.

We learn at once that 'Miss Brooke had that kind of beauty which seems to be thrown into relief by poor dress'.

But for quotations which are either interrogatory or exclamatory, punctuation marks should appear both before and after the closing quotation mark:

The pause is followed by Richard's demanding 'will no man say "Amen"?'.

Why does Shakespeare give Malcolm the banal question 'O, by whom?'?

When a short quotation is followed by a reference in parentheses, the final punctuation should follow the closing parenthesis:

He assumes the effect to be 'quite deliberate' (p. 29).

There is no reason to doubt the effect of this 'secret humiliation' (Book VI, Chapter 52).

The final full stop should precede the closing quotation mark only when a quotation forms a complete sentence (or sentences) and is not integrated within the preceding passage of introduction but is clearly separated from it.

(d) LONG QUOTATIONS

Long quotations (more than about sixty words of prose, prose quotations consisting of more than one paragraph even if less than sixty words, and verse quotations of more than two lines) should be broken off by an increased space from the preceding and following lines of typescript. They should not be enclosed within quotation marks. A quotation occurring within such a long quotation should be in single quotation marks; if a further quotation occurs within that, double quotation marks should be used. Foreign forms of quotation marks should not be preserved unless there are special reasons for doing so. Prose quotations should not be inset; verse quotations should be typed according to the lineation of the original and centred. These longer quotations should all be typed in double-spacing and they should be marked by a vertical line in the margin to indicate that they are to be printed in the form which is standard for the publication concerned.[1] Three forms in common use are (i) printing in a size of type smaller than that used for the main text, (ii) using the same type size as for the text but with reduced leading (line spacing), and (iii) using the same type size and leading as for the text but indenting. The preparation and marking of the typescript in the manner herein described would, however, be suitable for any likely method of printing (see Section 1 (k) above). If a quoted passage of prose begins a new paragraph in the original, it should start with the normal indention; otherwise the first line should be set full out. Long quotations should normally end with a full stop; even though the original may use other punctuation, there is no need (except for a question mark or exclamation mark) to preserve this at the end of a quotation. The initial letter of the first word of a quotation may also be changed to or from a capital if this is more appropriate in the context. A long quotation should never be used in the middle of a sentence of the main text: it is unreasonable to expect the reader to carry the sense of a sentence across a quotation several lines in length.

To assist the printer a long quotation should be marked in the margin 'verse' or 'prose' if there is any possibility of doubt.

Interpolations (indicating source) which necessitate the use of square brackets in the opening lines of long quotations (see first example below) should be avoided. Such interpolations can almost always be prevented by including the first words of the quotation in quotation marks in the preceding text (see second example). But a little rephrasing will often eliminate the need even for this (see third example):

---

[1] In dissertations, and other papers not intended for publication, long quotations may be typed with reduced spacing between lines.

This play [writes Dr Johnson, referring to *Cymbeline*] has many just sentiments, some natural dialogues, and some pleasing scenes, but they are obtained at the expense of much incongruity . . .

'This play', writes Dr Johnson, referring to *Cymbeline*,

has many just sentiments, some natural dialogues, and some pleasing scenes . . .

With reference to *Cymbeline*, Dr Johnson writes:

This play has many just sentiments, some natural dialogues, and some pleasing scenes . . .

A reference in brackets after a long quotation should always be placed outside the closing full stop, and without a full stop of its own.

(e) OMISSIONS

Omissions within prose quotations should be marked by an ellipsis (three spaced full stops). Omitted lines of verse should be marked by an ellipsis at the end of the line before the omission, and not by a row of dots across the page. It is not normally necessary to use an ellipsis at the beginning or end of a quotation; almost all quotations will be taken from a larger context and there is usually no need to indicate this obvious fact unless the sense of the passage quoted is manifestly incomplete. (See also section 4 (h) above.)

(f) COPYRIGHT

It is the responsibility of an author to obtain permission for the quotation of any copyright material if such permission appears to be necessary. Normally it is unnecessary to seek permission for the quotation of brief passages in a scholarly work.

It is not possible to give a definitive ruling to indicate when it is necessary to seek permission: copyright laws are not the same in all countries and different publishers hold varying views on the subject. In general it may be said that the length of the quoted passage and the use to which it is put should be fair to the original author and his publisher in that nothing is done to diminish the value of their publication.

C

The British Publishers' Association and the Society of Authors have suggested that there should be no need to seek permission if the following limits are not exceeded:

in prose: a single extract up to 400 words, or a series of extracts to a total of 800 words but of which no single extract exceeds 300 words;

in verse: an extract not exceeding 40 lines or one quarter of any poem.

Items such as illustrations or tables which are complete in themselves should not be reproduced without permission.

9
Footnotes

(a) GENERAL

(The term 'footnotes' is used throughout this section but the rules apply equally to notes and references printed at the end of an article, chapter, or book.)

Footnotes are an interruption to the reader and should be kept down to what is strictly necessary. They are intended primarily for documentation and for the citation of sources relevant to the text. They should not be used to provide additional bibliographical material on the general subject being treated, but not directly needed. Nor should they normally include extra expository material. Such material, if apposite and useful, is often better incorporated into the text, or added as an appendix. Only after the most careful consideration should it be included in footnotes.

All footnotes should end with full stops, whether or not they form complete sentences.

(b) METHODS OF LIMITING FOOTNOTES

Simple references (such as line numbers or page references to a book already cited in full) can usually be incorporated in the text, normally in parentheses after quotations. A string of footnote references to the same text can be avoided by stating after the first full footnote citation: 'Further references (to this edition, etc.) are given after quotations in the text.' (See also Section 10 (c).)

The number of footnotes can often be kept down by grouping together in one footnote references to several sources mentioned close together in the same paragraph. In particular, adjacent references to several pages of the same publication should be cited together in a single footnote. No footnote, however, should document references for more than one paragraph.

Footnotes should not repeat information already clear from the text: if, for example, the author has been named before a quotation there is no need to repeat the name in a footnote reference. If there is a bibliography to a book or article, footnotes can also be reduced (see Section 10 (a) below).

(c) POSITION AND NUMBERING

If possible a footnote reference number should be placed at the end of a sentence so as to interrupt the flow of the text as little as possible. Footnotes should be marked in the typescript by superior numbers, without punctuation (full stops, brackets, etc.), in sequence throughout an article or chapter. The editor (but not the author) should mark the numbers more clearly for the printer by encircling them in ink. A footnote reference number should follow any punctuation except a dash, which it should precede. It should appear at the end of a quotation, not following the author's name (if that precedes the quotation). A footnote reference number in the text should never be repeated to refer to the same footnote; if the same material has to be referred to again, a new note in the form 'See note 1 above' should be used. Footnote numbers in headings and subheadings are to be avoided; an asterisk may, however, be used to indicate a general note to an entire article or chapter.

10

References

(a) GENERAL

References (in the body of an article or chapter, or in footnotes) should document the information offered, to allow the reader, if he wishes, to check the evidence on which an argument is based. A reference must therefore enable the reader to find the source referred to as quickly and easily as possible.

A work should be quoted or referred to in a satisfactory scholarly edition. If a work is published both in Great Britain and overseas, the British edition should be used unless there are special reasons to the contrary. If an edition other than the first is used (because the later edition is revised, for instance), this should be stated. If an unrevised reprint is used (for example a modern facsimile reprint of an out-of-print work or a paperbound reissue of an earlier book), the publication details of the original edition, as well as of the reprint, should be given. This is especially necessary if articles from learned journals are used in anthologies of criticism ('Casebooks' etc.): a reader looking for the article in a library is more likely to find the original journal than the anthology. In referring to works of literature of which several editions may be available, it is often helpful to give the reader more information than merely the page number of the edition used:

p. 235 (Book iii, Chapter 4)

and in quoting a letter:

p. 281 (23 April 1864)

Full references to well-known works (*OED*, *DNB*, etc.) are normally unnecessary, though for encyclopaedias and biographical dictionaries of multiple authorship it is often relevant to name the writer of the article cited.

In a book or article which contains a bibliography of works cited there is usually no need to give full publication details in the footnotes; the author's or editor's name and the title of the article or book will normally be sufficient, together with a reference to the page or pages referred to. (The reader should be referred to the bibliography after the first footnote citation in this abbreviated form.) But the date of publication may occasionally be relevant to the argument. Care should be taken to check all footnote references against the bibliography.

The use of inelegant (and possibly ambiguous) abbreviations in references should be avoided. Use 'translated by' not 'tr.', 'revised by' not 'rev.', 'edited by' not 'ed.', etc. Do not use 'cf.' or 'cp.' when you mean simply 'see'; and when the sense of 'compare' is intended, the English word in full is preferable. In general, latinate abbreviations in references should be avoided when there is an acceptable alternative.

(b) FORMS OF REFERENCE

(i) BOOKS

The first reference should be given in full in a form similar to that of the following examples:

1. Joseph G. Price, *The Unfortunate Comedy: A Study of 'All's Well that Ends Well' and its Critics* (Liverpool, 1968), p. 59.

2. Joan Bennett, *Four Metaphysical Poets*, second edition (London, 1953), p. 30.

3. James Sutherland, *Defoe*, Writers and their Work, 51 (London, 1954), p. 23.

4. *The Works of William Fowler*, edited by Henry W. Meikle, James Craigie, and John Purves, Scottish Text Society, 3 vols (Edinburgh and London, 1914–40), III, 94–98.

5. *The Works of Thomas Nashe*, edited by R. B. McKerrow, second edition, revised by F. P. Wilson, 5 vols (Oxford, 1958), III, 129.

6. *The Works of Samuel Johnson*, Volume VI, *Poems*, edited by R. L. McAdam, Jr, with George Milne (New Haven, Connecticut, 1968), p. 201.

7. Niccolò Machiavelli, *The Chief Works and Others*, translated by Allan Gilbert, 3 vols (Durham, North Carolina, 1965), I, 9.

8. Peter Pawlowsky, *Helmut Küpper vormals Georg Bondi, 1895–1970* (Munich, 1970), p. 12.

9. *Essays on Shakespeare and Elizabethan Drama: In Honour of Hardin Craig*, edited by Richard Hosley (London, 1963), pp. 41–49.

10. *Correspondance complète de Jean Jacques Rousseau*, edited by R. A. Leigh (Geneva, 1965–), V (1967), 107–08 (5 July 1758).

That is:

Author (forenames or initials preceding surname)

Full title (in italics), including dedicatee if the work is a *Festschrift*

Editor, translator, or compiler (if any)

Name of series in which book appears (if any) and volume number in that series; not italicized or in quotation marks

Edition, if other than the first

Number of volumes (if more than one)

Place of publication (name of town, and country or state if necessary), year(s) of publication; these details are enclosed in parentheses

Volume number (if any), in small capital roman numerals, followed where necessary (see below) by year of publication of that volume in parentheses

Page number(s) on which the material cited occurs

The last item is followed by a full stop; all other items are followed by a comma unless they precede a parenthesis.

If there is no volume number, 'p.' or 'pp.' should be inserted before the page number(s) to avoid ambiguity; it should rarely be necessary to use 'vol.' before the volume number.

The forms of authors' and editors' names should be given in full as printed on the title-page. Forenames or initials should precede surnames. (Only in an alphabetical bibliography do surnames appear first.) The names of up to three authors should be given in full; for works by more than three authors the name of only the first should be given, followed by 'and others'. If the author's name is more conveniently included within the title (as, for example, in editions of 'works'), or if the book is an edited collection or anthology, the title will appear first (see examples 4 to 6, 9, and 10). If an entry relates to several successive pages, the first and last page numbers should always be stated:

pp. 278–309 *not* pp. 278 ff.

The wording of the title should be as on the title-page, though very long titles should be suitably abbreviated. A colon (not a comma or semi-colon) should be used to separate title and sub-title, even though lineation on the title-page itself may obviate the need for this mark to appear there (see examples 1 and 9). Capitalization of titles should follow the rules given in Section 5 (d) above. If figures occur in titles, these should also be italicized (see example 8). If an italicized title includes within it another title, this should be enclosed in single quotation marks (see example 1). For books (usually older works) with alternative titles, punctuation before and after 'or' should be as follows:

The Queen; or, The Excellency of Her Sex
All for Love; or, The World Well Lost

A reference to a work in several volumes published over a period of years but now complete should state the number of volumes and give inclusive dates of publication and the date of the volume specifically referred to where this is not the first or last in the series. But if a work in several volumes is incomplete and still in process of publication, the number of volumes cannot of course be given; the date of the first volume should be stated, followed by a dash, and the date of the individual volume being cited should be added in parentheses after the volume number (see example 10). In some instances (for example if each volume of a set has a different editor) it may be more appropriate to give publication details only for the volume cited (see example 6).

Any detail of publication (place, date, etc.) which is uncertain or not given in the book itself should be enclosed in square brackets. Do not use square brackets for any other purpose (for example, when the reference is already in parentheses), otherwise the impression will be conveyed that the information in square brackets is uncertain.

The name of the publisher should be given only if a reference would be otherwise inadequate (e.g. if it might not be possible to distinguish between different editions) or if it is required by the editorial policy of the publication in which the reference will appear.

In giving the place of publication, the English forms of the names of towns (Vienna, Milan, Munich, etc.) should be used (see Section 2 (f) above and Section 10 (f) below).

London and Paris should be included as places of publication unless (as, for example, in a bibliographical article) there are likely to be a great many references to books published at one place. In these circumstances, provide an early footnote in the form 'Place of publication of all books cited is London (or Paris, etc.) unless otherwise stated'.

If an edition other than the first is being cited, this must be made clear by including the words 'second (or third, etc.) edition' immediately before the place and date of publication (see examples 2 and 5).

(ii) ARTICLES IN BOOKS

Examples of first references:

1. James L. Smith, '*The Jew of Malta* in the Theatre', in *Christopher Marlowe*, edited by Brian Morris, Mermaid Critical Commentaries (London, 1968), pp. 3–23.
2. Daniel Seltzer, 'The Staging of the Last Plays', in *Later Shakespeare*, edited by John Russell Brown and Bernard Harris, Stratford-upon-Avon Studies, 8 (London, 1966), pp. 81–101 (p. 95).

That is:

Author of article

Title of article (in single quotation marks)

The word 'in' followed by title and publication details of book as in Section 10 (b) (i) above

First and last page numbers of the article cited

Page number(s), in parentheses, of the particular reference (if necessary)

The last item is followed by a full stop; all other items are followed by a comma unless they precede a parenthesis.

The titles of works of literature occurring within the titles of articles should be italicized (as in the first example) or placed within quotation marks, whichever is appropriate (see Section 6 (c) above). If quotation marks are appropriate they should be double, since single quotation marks will already have been used for the title of the article.

If a particular page within an article is to be indicated, the first and last pages should nevertheless be given in the first full citation and a reference to the particular page added in parentheses (as in the second example).

Other subdivisions in books, when separately cited, should be treated as seems appropriate according to this general pattern. Thus:

James Shirley, *The Triumph of Peace*, edited by Clifford Leech, in *A Book of Masques: In Honour of Allardyce Nicoll*, edited by T. J. B. Spencer and S. W. Wells (London, 1967), pp. 277–305 (p. 293).

(iii) ARTICLES IN JOURNALS

Examples of first references:

1. Jonas Barish, 'Ovid, Juvenal, and *The Silent Woman*', *PMLA*, 71 (1956), 213–24 (p. 219).
2. C. C. Clarke, 'A Note on "To be or not to be"', *Essays in Criticism*, 10 (1960), 18–23 (p. 20).
3. Christopher Ricks, 'Tennyson: "Armageddon" into "Timbuctoo"', *MLR*, 61 (1966), 23–24.

That is:

Author's name

Title of article, in single quotation marks

Title of journal, in italics

Volume number, in arabic numerals

Year of publication, in parentheses

First and last page numbers of the article cited

Page number(s), in parentheses, of the particular reference (if necessary)

The last item is followed by a full stop; all other items are followed by a comma unless they precede a parenthesis.

Only the main title, not the sub-title, of a journal should be given. An initial '*The*' or '*A*' should be omitted. If the title is abbreviated to initials, full stops should not be used (see Section 3 (d) above). The titles of journals should be abbreviated only when the abbreviation is likely to be familiar to all readers, otherwise the title should be given in full. If there are to be several references to the same journal, an abbreviated title should be indicated after the first full reference or in a preliminary list of abbreviations. For the proceedings of learned societies, etc., the name of the organization should be italicized as part of the title:

Proceedings of the British Academy (*not* British Academy, *Proceedings*)

The titles of works of literature occurring within the titles of articles, and references to particular pages within an article, are, as the examples indicate, treated in the same way as for articles in books (see Section 10 (b) (ii) above).

Normally the month or season of publication of a journal, or the part number, will not be necessary to a reference, and should be omitted. But where a journal has individual parts or monthly issues separately paginated, the date and number will be necessary:

Lionel Trilling, 'In Mansfield Park', *Encounter*, 3, no. 3 (September 1954), 9–19 (p. 12).

W. H. Auden, 'Plains', *London Magazine*, 1, no. 3 (April 1954), 13–15.

(iv) ARTICLES IN NEWSPAPERS

References to articles in daily or weekly newspapers require only the date of issue (day, month, and year) and the page number or numbers; volume or part numbers should not be included. Only the main title of the newspaper should be given, and initial '*The*' or '*A*' is normally omitted (though it is customary to write '*The Times*' in full). Otherwise the method of citation is the same as for other articles (see Sections 10 (b) (ii) and (iii) above):

1. Anthony Powell, 'Proust the Soldier', *The Times*, 3 July 1971, p. 5.
2. A. S. Bell, 'The Walter Scott Manuscripts in the National Library of Scotland', *TLS*, 9 July 1971, p. 813.

(v) DISSERTATIONS AND THESES

The titles of unpublished dissertations should be in roman type within single quotation marks, followed by the degree (where known), university, and date in parentheses:

James-Louis Boyle, 'Marcel Proust et les écrivains anglais' (unpublished dissertation, University of Paris, 1953), p. 22.

Diedrich Diederichsen, 'Shakespeare und das deutsche Märchendrama' (unpublished doctoral dissertation, University of Hamburg, 1952), p. 91.

Robert J. Fusillo, 'The Staging of Battle Scenes on the Shakespearian Stage' (unpublished Ph.D. dissertation, University of Birmingham, 1966), p. 86.

If a published abstract of an unpublished dissertation is known to exist, the information should be given.

(vi) PLAYS AND LONG POEMS

After the first full reference to the edition used (see Section 10 (b) (i) above), later references, wherever possible incorporated after quotations within the text (see Section 9 (b) above), should be given as:

The Merchant of Venice, II. 3. 10; *The Faerie Queene*, IV. 26. 35; *Paradise Lost*, IX. 342; *Samson Agonistes*, line (*or* l.) 819 (meaning, in each case, that the line is the first line of the quotation). It is unnecessary to give a closing line number when a sequence of consecutive lines is quoted. The form 'IV. 2. 210–23' should be used when a passage is referred to but not quoted. If there are substantial omissions in the lines quoted, the form 'IV. 3. 412, 423', meaning that the quotation begins at line 412 and that there is an omission before line 423, should generally be sufficient. The omission will also be marked in the text (see Section 8 (e) above).

Small capital roman numerals should be used for the numbers of acts of plays, and for the numbers of 'books' and other major subdivisions. Smaller subdivisions (scenes, cantos, chapters, etc.) and line numbers are usually indicated by arabic numerals. Figures in references should be separated by full stops (not commas).

(vii) THE BIBLE

References should be in the following form: Isaiah 22. 17; II Corinthians 5. 13–15. Note that books of the Bible are not italicized; roman numerals are used for the numbers of books, arabic numerals (separated by a full stop) for chapters and verses.

(viii) MANUSCRIPTS

Names of repositories and collections should be given in full in the first instance and an abbreviated form should be used for subsequent references. The degree of abbreviation which may be acceptable will depend upon the frequency with which a particular repository, collection, or manuscript is referred to. The names of manuscript collections should be given in roman type without quotation marks and the citation of manuscripts within collections should be according to the system of classification of the repository. For Public Record Office manuscripts it is sufficient to give the call number alone for all references except the first.

The following examples show the method of citation both for first and later references. Note that, because of the danger of ambiguity, the abbreviations 'fol.' and 'fols' are preferred to 'f.' and 'ff.'.

First reference: British Library, Cotton MSS, Caligula D III, fol. 15

Later references: BL, Cotton MSS, Caligula D III, fols 17–18

        or: Cotton MSS, Caligula D III, fols 17–18

First reference: Paris, Bibliothèque Nationale, fonds français, 1124

Later references: BN, f. fr. 1124

First reference: Sheffield Central Library, Fitzwilliam MS E.209

Later references: Sheffield CL, Fitzwilliam MS E.151

First reference: Public Record Office, Home Office, HO 42/196

Later references: PRO, HO 42/196

(c) LATER REFERENCES

In all references to a book or article after the first, the shortest intelligible form should be used. This will normally be the author's name followed by the page reference:

Quiller-Couch, p. 79.

If no ambiguity is possible use the page reference alone. (It is preferable that this should be included in parentheses within the text rather than as a footnote; see Section 9 (b) above.) Sometimes it may be necessary, for example when more than one work by an author has been cited, to repeat a title or a shortened form of a title:

Quiller-Couch, *On the Art of Reading*, p. 79.

If there can be no doubt which author is referred to but more than one of his works is being quoted, use the title of the specific work (or short title if the full title has already been given) followed by the page reference:

On the Art of Reading, p. 79; or *Art of Reading*, p. 79.

Such phrases as 'loc. cit.', 'op. cit.', 'ibid.', etc., unless used with precise care and accuracy, will confuse the reader. Since they are only marginally more economical of space than the unambiguous repetition of the name of the author of the work or the short title, they should be avoided.

(d) CITATION BY THE AUTHOR–DATE SYSTEM

The method of quoting references described in Section 10 (a) to (c) above is recommended for use in the humanities but a different system is commonly used in other disciplines — notably in the sciences. This method admits footnotes only in exceptional circumstances and is often referred to as the Author–Date System. All references are placed at the end of each individual paper of a multi-author work. If the work is by a single author the references may appear at the end of each chapter or, arranged by chapters, at the end of the book. References in the text give the surname of the author (or authors) of the work to which reference is made, followed by the date of publication. This information is enclosed in parentheses as in the following examples:

> Certain alloys, when exposed to specific environments, fail under the continued action of low stresses (Swann 1981).

> Some investigators (Fitton and Smith 1979; Brown 1980) have found that these theories have not proved reliable.

When it is necessary to draw attention to a particular page or pages this may be done thus:

> The building is not accepted as Anglo-Saxon (Taylor and Taylor 1965, 159–60, 283–84).

If two or more works by the same author have the same publication date they should be distinguished by adding letters after the date:

> Unmistakable evidence of a medieval field-system was found here (Markston 1952 b).

The list of references is arranged in alphabetical order of the authors' surnames. This reference list differs from a normal bibliography (see sub-section (f) below) in that the date of publication follows the author's name instead of following the place of publication. This arrangement makes it easier for the reader to relate the textual reference (author, date) to the final list of references. Other points to be noted are:

1.   the name of the place of publication of books need not be in parentheses but should be separated from the title of the work by a comma;

2.   titles of books or journals are printed in italics; abbreviated titles may be used for publications which are likely to be well known to the

reader; titles of articles are printed in roman type and are not enclosed in quotation marks;

3. the words 'editor' and 'edited' may be abbreviated to 'ed.';

4. if the work cited is an article in a book or journal the first and last page numbers of the article should be given;

5. if the list includes more than one work by the same author a long dash should be substituted for his name after the first appearance.

Examples are given below:

Angus, J. A., 1901	*The Angles in Scotland*, Edinburgh
Jackson, D., 1978	The Skiddaw Group, *The Geology of the Lake District*, ed. F. Moseley, Leeds, pp. 79–98
Leeds, E. T., 1923	A Saxon Village near Sutton Courtenay, *Archaeologia*, 73, pp. 147–92
———— 1968	*Early Anglo-Saxon Art and Archaeology*, Oxford
Markston, A. W., 1952 a	*Scandinavian Influence in the Yorkshire Dales*, London
———— 1952 b	Early Medieval Settlement in Pikedale, *Yorkshire History*, 12, pp. 112–24
Rodwell, W., 1976	The Archaeological Investigation of Hadstock Church, *Antiq. J.*, 56, pp. 55–71

If unpublished documents are referred to, an abbreviated form of reference should appear in parentheses in the text and a separate list should appear at the end of the paper preceding or following the list of published sources (which may include unpublished theses since they have specific authors). The items in the list should be arranged in systematic (e.g. alphabetical) order. The following examples illustrate, in the left-hand column, the abbreviations used in the text and, in the right-hand column, the full references:

BL Bib. Reg. 18 D III	British Library, Royal Books, Report to Lord Burghley on the western border, 1590
CRO, Probate	Cumberland Record Office, Carlisle Castle, Probate Records
NLS 6118	National Library of Scotland, Edinburgh, Armstrong MS 6118
PRO Prob11	Public Record Office, Probate Office, wills

(e) CROSS-REFERENCES

Avoid, as far as possible, cross-references within an article or book. The page numbers in the printed article or book will not, of course, coincide with those in the typescript, and numerous references of this kind will therefore involve considerable extra work for author, editor, and printer, and will increase the possibility of error. Cross-references to pages can sometimes be avoided by giving references to chapters, sections, or notes, if the notes are numbered consecutively throughout each chapter or article: 'See Chapter 3', 'See Chapter 4, note 7'. (For the treatment of cross-references, if they are necessary, see Section 1 (n) above.)

(f) BIBLIOGRAPHIES

In an alphabetical bibliography the surname of the author or editor whose surname governs the alphabetical position will precede his forename or initials. But there is no need to reverse the normal order for collaborating authors or editors. The words 'editor' and 'edited' may here be abbreviated to 'ed.'. The following examples illustrate these points:

Donno, E. S., ed., *Elizabethan Minor Epics* (London, 1963)
Keats, John, *Poems*, ed. by Miriam Allott (London, 1970)
Thomas, R. H., and Wilfried Van der Will, *The German Novel and the Affluent Society* (Manchester, 1968)
Gravett, K. W. E., 'Brookland Belfry', *Archaeologia Cantiana*, 89 (1974), 43–48

Other abbreviations (such as the omission of London or Paris as a place of publication with a general note to this effect) may be appropriate. If preferred, the parentheses enclosing details of publication may be omitted, and the title and the place of publication separated by a comma. Consistency, however, is essential. In a bibliography in list form, final full stops after each item should not be used. In a long bibliography of foreign books the native forms of the places of publication are sometimes preferable; and if formal bibliographical descriptions of books are being given, as, for example, in review headings, the spelling of the place of publication should be as given on the title-page. It may be helpful to state the number of text pages in a book at the conclusion of an entry; the length of articles will of course be clear from the citation of first and last pages as part of the entry.

II

Presentation of Theses and Dissertations

(a) GENERAL

The requirements of universities and colleges for the presentation and layout of theses and dissertations vary in matters of detail. The following general recommendations will be applicable to most literary theses, but should be supplemented by reference to the particular regulations and requirements of the university or college in which the thesis is to be presented; candidates must, therefore, be in possession of a current list of such local requirements before a thesis is prepared for presentation.

Few institutions require that a thesis should be presented in printed form, and the comments that follow apply primarily to theses which will be presented in typescript. They are offered on the assumption that recommendations in earlier parts of this *Style Book* have been followed before preparation of the final typescript begins.

(b) THE LENGTH OF THE THESIS

Local regulations vary considerably on the permitted lengths of theses and these regulations must be consulted and observed. The total length normally refers to the number of words in the main text and appendices, but usually excludes preliminary matter, notes, bibliography, and index. If a text is being edited the word-limit normally excludes the text itself but includes all explanatory notes, glossary, introduction, appendices, etc.

(c) PARTS OF THE THESIS

(i) TITLE-PAGE

The title should be a concise and accurate description of the content of the thesis. The title-page should also give the full name of the author, the qualification for which the thesis is submitted, the name of the university in which it is submitted, and the date (month and year). Many institutions have a prescribed form of words for the title-page, which must be followed. If the thesis is in more than one volume, the number of volumes should be given on the title-page of the first volume and later volumes should have their own title-pages with the particular volume-number specified.

(ii) SUMMARY OR SYNOPSIS

Local regulations are often precise and strict about the position, length, and form of the synopsis. It is frequently required to follow the title-page. Unless other regulations apply it should not exceed five hundred words. An accurate and concise summary of the organization and content of the thesis is normally required. The scope of the work undertaken, the method of investigation, the main divisions of the thesis, and the conclusions reached should all be described. The contribution made by the thesis to knowledge of the subject treated should be clearly stated, without either undue modesty or ostentation. Many institutions require that the synopsis should also include a statement of the total number of words contained in the thesis.

(iii) TABLE OF CONTENTS AND LIST OF ILLUSTRATIONS

Any preliminary sections following the table of contents, chapter and appendix numbers and titles, bibliography, and index should all be listed, with page references. Titles should agree exactly with their wording in the main text of the thesis. The listing of smaller sub-divisions within chapters is not normally necessary, especially if the thesis has an index; if included in the table of contents, however, such subheadings should be listed in full, and consistently throughout all chapters and sections. If a thesis is bound in more than one volume, the contents of the whole thesis should be listed in the first volume; each subsequent volume should begin with a list of its own contents.

A list, or lists, of plates, diagrams, tables, etc. should follow the table of contents and should also give the page references. For a plate, or for any full-page illustration or table which does not itself bear a page-number, this reference should be to the number of the page preceding the item in question.

(iv) PREFACE, ACKNOWLEDGEMENTS, DECLARATION

If local regulations do not require a synopsis, a preface, serving a similar function, may usefully follow the list of contents. A parade of other preliminary matter is usually inappropriate in a scholarly thesis: acknowledgements of specific instances of assistance are frequently better placed in a note at the relevant point in the text; acknowledgement of permission to reproduce illustrations, quotations, etc. should appear with the material concerned; general assistance of the kind inevitable in any academic work — from librarians, supervisor, and friends — may normally go unacknowledged in an unpublished thesis unless there are special reasons to the contrary.

When a thesis contains material that the author has already published (or used in an earlier thesis), this should be acknowledged in a preliminary declaration. If the thesis is based on joint research, the nature and extent of the candidate's individual contribution should also be indicated here.

(v) LIST OF ABBREVIATIONS

Abbreviations (of titles etc.) regularly used throughout a thesis should be listed, with a key, immediately before the first page of the main text (see also Section 3 above). The first use of an abbreviation in the text should refer the reader to the preliminary key.

(vi) TEXT

Theses should be divided into sections, chapters, and subsections as may be appropriate. The first section or chapter will normally take the form of an introduction, placing the thesis in relation to its general topic and to other work in the subject. Section and chapter titles, and subheadings, should be factual, concise, and descriptively accurate.

(vii) NOTES

Unless local regulations specify otherwise, notes should be numbered in a single sequence throughout each chapter (or section), but with a separate sequence for each chapter. The note reference numbers within the text should be typed above the line without punctuation. Notes may be placed either at the foot of each page (and may then be in reduced spacing), or at the end of each chapter, or, grouped by chapter, in one section at the end of the thesis, immediately before the bibliography. The choice should be made with regard to the nature of the dissertation, local regulations, and the supervisor's advice.

(viii) APPENDICES

Material, such as lists, tables, copies of documents, and other supporting information, which would constitute too great an interruption of the main text and is too extensive to be included in the notes, may sometimes be offered in one or more appendices. (The proliferation of appendices, however, and the inclusion of material of doubtful relevance, is to be avoided.)

(ix) BIBLIOGRAPHY

Almost every literary thesis will contain a bibliography. This should not be compiled as a last-minute task before submission of the thesis, but will develop from the material being listed, consulted, and used while work is in progress. The degree of inclusiveness of a bibliography is a matter for careful consideration and consultation with a supervisor: it should include all works found relevant, and must detail all works referred to in the text. Full publication details will be included (see Section 10 (f) above). The list will normally be in alphabetical order of authors, though in certain theses a chronological, or some other, order may be more appropriate. Some degree of subdivision within the bibliography is frequently desirable. Manuscript and printed material should always be separately listed. Other subdivisions might be into primary and secondary sources, general works and special studies, or any other arrangement that may be appropriate.

It is advisable to hold a bibliography in card-index form until the latest possible moment before typing, so that rearrangements and additions can be made.

(x) INDEX

Although not always required by local regulations, the provision of an index of names (and if possible of subjects) is frequently worthwhile, particularly for theses covering a wide range of material or concerned with the work of several authors. An index also is best held in card form until the latest possible moment; page references may then be added to cards when the final typing of the text is complete.

(d) PREPARATION OF THE FINAL TYPESCRIPT

(i) GENERAL

Adequate time must be allowed for preparation, typing, checking, correction, and (where necessary) retyping. The typing should commence as soon as possible since a thesis in a unique manuscript (or draft typescript) bears a serious risk of loss. If sections are being put into their final form as composition of the thesis proceeds, fair copies should be made as each section is completed. An entire thesis should never be given to a typist without some provision for checking while typing is in progress. Immediate examination of the first sections typed is essential so that recurrent problems and difficulties can be identified and prevented in later stages. Before any section of a thesis is handed over to a typist, all references and quotations should be verified and a thorough check made of the sequence of footnote numbers, both of the reference numbers in the text and of the numbers of the notes themselves.

(ii) PAPER, TYPE FACE, AND MARGINS

Unless local regulations specify otherwise, theses should be typed on one side only of white paper of A4 size and good quality. Both 'pica' and 'élite' type sizes are normally acceptable, provided that typing is of even size throughout and characters clear and black. Margins should be $1\frac{1}{2}$ inches (4 cm) wide at the left-hand side (for binding) and three quarters of an inch (2 cm) on the other three sides. The typing should be reasonably consistent in the length of line and the number of lines per page. If a typewriter has an italic type face this may be used for titles, foreign words and phrases, etc. (see Section 6 above), but underlining is normally acceptable.

(iii) SPACING

The text, preliminaries, and appendices should be typed in double spacing throughout. Single spacing is usually acceptable for longer quotations (see Section 8 above) and for notes. The bibliography and index will probably require a special tabular presentation; double spacing between items and single spacing within items is often a convenient layout here.

(iv) PAGINATION

Unless local regulations stipulate otherwise, page numbers should begin on the first page of the main text (following the preliminaries) and continue to the end, and should be placed at the top of each page.

(v) HEADINGS AND SUBHEADINGS

Chapters (and other main sections) should always begin on a new page; their titles should be in capitals and centred. Subsections should not begin on a new page, but should be marked by extra spacing; more important subheadings should be on a separate line and in capitals, but set over to the left-hand margin; minor subheadings, also set to the left and on a separate line, should have only initial capitals and should be underlined. No punctuation marks should be used after headings and subheadings. If a system of designation by letters and numerals is required for subsections, one based on the descending order given in Section 1 (f) above may be used.

(vi) CHECKING AND CORRECTION

Thorough checking of the final typescript is essential. It should be checked word for word and letter for letter against the verified copy given to the typist; quotations and references should again be checked against the originals; note numbers should be checked; and the typescript should be read through at least once more, preferably by someone other than the author. Only the smallest corrections should be made by hand (in black ink); all corrections of more than a letter or so should be typed in. Some corrections may well involve the retyping of a whole page, or more, and adequate time must therefore be allowed for checking and correction.

(vii) CROSS-REFERENCES

Unless a thesis is divided into many small subsections, page numbers will normally be essential for cross-references. These cannot, therefore, be included until typing and pagination are complete. The author, however, will normally be able to guess whether a two-digit or three-digit number has to be inserted, and should make it clear to the typist how many spaces have to be left for the number to be typed in at the final stage. Since the task of inserting cross-references is troublesome, they should be kept to an absolute minimum. If the need for frequent cross-referencing emerges during the earlier stages of composition of a thesis, the overall structure may be at fault and a remedy should be sought before the preparation of the final typescript.

(viii) ILLUSTRATIONS

Illustrations (especially photographic plates, and tables or large illustrations which have to be folded) may cause difficulties with binding; the advice of the binder should be sought at an early stage if illustrations are likely to be numerous. Local requirements for the mounting of illustrations should be carefully observed; a binding margin of at least the usual $1\frac{1}{2}$ inches (4 cm) will be required. If possible, illustrations should be inserted in the thesis near the relevant portion of the text. There should be a separate numbering sequence for each category of illustration (plates, figures, tables, etc.). Numbers and captions should appear below the illustration. If an illustration has to be turned in order to be mounted on A4 paper, its left-hand side should be to the bottom of the page of the bound thesis. The process of obtaining several copies of an illustration can be surprisingly slow, and adequate time must be allowed.

(ix) NUMBER OF COPIES

Local regulations vary on the number of copies of a thesis to be presented and on whether one copy is returned to the candidate after the thesis has been examined. Good quality carbon copies are normally acceptable, but xerographic copies made from the finally corrected typescript save a good deal of trouble in both the typing and correcting stages and may be preferable.

(e) BINDING

Nearly every university and college requires that theses should be bound in boards; some require this binding to be delayed until after the thesis has been examined, others require binding to be completed before submission. Local regulations on style of binding, and lettering on the front board (if any) and spine (usually at least the name of the candidate, the degree, and the year) must be observed. Binding delays are not infrequent, especially in university library binderies near the yearly or half-yearly date for submission of theses, and adequate time must, once again, be allowed.

(f) PERMISSION TO CONSULT AND COPY

Many universities and colleges now require the authors of theses deposited in their libraries to sign a declaration granting to the librarian the right to permit, without further reference to the author, consultation of the thesis and the making of single copies (for study purposes, and subject to the usual conventions of scholarly acknowledgement) of all or of parts of it. As always it is essential to be aware of current regulations in the institution to which the thesis is being submitted.

(g) FURTHER READING

The following may be found useful.

British Standards Institution, *BS 4821: Recommendations for the Presentation of Theses* (London, 1972)

George Watson, *The Literary Thesis: A Guide to Research* (London, 1970)

12

Glossary

The entries include only those words which are likely to be useful to an author or editor. The glossary does not purport to be a complete list of printers' technical terms.

art paper: a smooth, coated paper used for printing fine screen halftone illustrations.

bleed: if an illustration runs slightly beyond the edge of a page so that a small part is cut away when the book is trimmed, it is said to bleed, or to be *bled off*.

block: a relief printing surface, normally used to reproduce an illustration. It is usually made of metal and produced by photography and chemical etching.

blockmaker's proof: a proof of a block printed on good coated paper by the blockmaker. This accurately reproduces the quality of the block whereas the printer's proof is only intended to show the position and the caption.

body: the metal shank of a piece of type which serves as a base for the printing face. Type sizes are expressed in points (q.v.) measuring from head to foot on the body or shank. Type faces of different design can, however, appear to be of different sizes (see *x height* below) even if their body size is the same.

camera copy: artwork, type-proofs, etc. ready to be photographed for reproduction.

caps: capital letters.

caret: a sign marking the place in a text where additional material is to be inserted.

cold composition: literally any method of typesetting which does not use hot metal. It may therefore refer to photosetting (q.v.) or to some form of typewriter setting but is most commonly used of the latter.

copy: material, usually in the form of manuscript or typescript, to be set in type or otherwise prepared for printing.

diacritical marks: accents, bars, dots, etc. printed above or below letters.

ellipsis: three spaced full stops used to indicate an omission.

em: the square of any type size, therefore an em in 8-point type is 8 points wide. The type areas for a page are always calculated in 12 point (pica) ems (see *point* below).

em rule: a rule which is one em wide, a long dash (see Section 4 (b)).

en: half the width of an em (q.v.); also used in casting-off (estimating the length of a manuscript) to mean the average width of all characters and spaces, although this may not be equal to an en of the type size.

endmatter: material following the text proper, including appendices, bibliographies, indexes, etc.

endnotes: notes which appear at the end of chapters or at the end of a book, as opposed to footnotes.

en rule: a rule which is one en wide, a short dash (see Section 4 (b)).

figure: an illustration printed with the text (a *plate* is printed separately).

filmsetting (see *photosetting*).

foldout: a leaf larger than the normal page size which is folded to fit within the size of the book. It usually displays a large illustration or table.

folio: (1) a sheet of manuscript or typescript; (2) a page-number in a book; (3) a standard-size sheet folded in half, hence a book of this size.

format: the page size and shape of a book: sometimes loosely used to denote also the design.

forme: several pages of type and/or blocks fastened in a metal frame (a chase); usually in multiples of four (8 pp., 16 pp., 32 pp.).

fount: (pronounced *font*) a set of type characters of the same size and design. It may include capitals, small capitals, lower case, numerals, punctuation marks, and other sorts (q.v.).

full point: printer's term for a period or full stop.

galley proof: a proof printed from type which is contained in a long metal tray known as a galley. This is normally the first proof to be prepared and it displays the text in a long column. At a later stage the type is divided into pages but may be retained on the galley so that the next proof would be 'page on galley'.

guillemets: quotation marks used in French and some other languages (« »).

halftone: a process whereby an illustration is photographically broken up into a fine grid of dots of varying size. When printed (either by letterpress or lithography) this simulates the varying tones of the original.

hot-metal typesetting: the setting and casting of type from molten metal using machines such as the Monotype and the Linotype.

inferior: a small numeral or letter which is printed below or partly below the base line of a full-size character.

ISBN: International Standard Book Number: a number which identifies a particular book in accordance with an international system.

justify: to space out lines of type to a particular measure by varying the space between words.

landscape: a book or part of a book (e.g. an illustration or a table) which has a width greater than its height. See also *portrait*.

leaders: a row of evenly spaced dots designed to lead the reader's eye from one column of words or figures to another.

leading: introducing space between lines of type which is additional to that provided by the body of the type. This can be done by inserting thin strips of lead alloy between the lines of type but is more often effected by setting the type face on a larger than normal body (q.v.).

letterpress: the process of printing from raised surfaces such as type and engraved blocks.

letterspacing: the insertion of very thin spaces between the letters of a word. This is normally done only if the word is in capitals or small capitals.

ligature: two or more letters joined together as a single piece of type; common examples are: fi, fl, ffi, and ffl.

line drawing: a drawing which has no variation of tone or shade but consists only of monotone lines and solids.

lining figures: arabic numerals of constant height, e.g. 1234567, as opposed to non-lining (or old style) figures, e.g. 1234567.

lithography: a process of printing based on the mutual repulsion of grease and water. The printing surface is not raised, as in letterpress printing, but is a flat image laid down on a grained stone or plate. A film of water is applied which covers the surface of the stone or plate but is rejected by the image. When the plate is inked the ink adheres to the image but is repelled by the damp surface of the remainder of the plate, so that only the image prints.

make-up: the arrangement of type lines and illustrations into page form.

measure: the width (usually expressed in 12 point ems) to which lines of type are set.

Monotype: a typesetting system which consists of two machines — a keyboard producing a punched paper tape and a caster which is controlled by the paper tape and produces single type characters.

offprint: an article or other excerpt from a book or journal run on (q.v.) from the main printing run and bound separately.

offset-lithography: common method of printing by lithography (q.v.) in which the image is first transferred from the plate on to a rubber-covered cylinder whence it is printed on to the paper.

over-running: the transferring of words from one line of type to the next or to the preceding line to accommodate a correction. Such a correction may mean over-running as far as the end of a paragraph. In an extreme case this could affect many subsequent pages.

page proof: a proof printed from type which has been divided into pages, with running heads (q.v.) and footnotes in position; this is usually the final proof, on which corrections made to the galley proof (q.v.) can be checked but to which no further correction should be made.

parentheses: round brackets ( ).

perfect binding: a method of binding a book or journal without stitching or sewing. The signatures (q.v.) are assembled and their backs cut off. The resulting edge is then covered with an adhesive. Usually a paper cover is attached and the remaining three edges are trimmed.

photolithography: the process of printing by lithography (q.v.) when the plate is prepared photographically from positive or negative film.

photo-offset: offset-lithography (q.v.) where the printing plate has been prepared by a photographic process.

photosetting: setting by a machine which produces the image of the characters photographically on bromide paper or film, as distinct from *typesetting* which implies the use of metal type.

pica: twelve points (see *point* below). A unit of typographic measurement used in the English-speaking countries. A pica (or 12 point em) is approximately one-sixth of an inch and 'measure' (q.v.) is normally expressed in picas.

plate: (1) an illustration printed on a separate sheet of paper from the text; most frequently a halftone (q.v.) printed on glossy coated (art) paper; plates can be inserted in or wrapped round signatures (q.v.), or tipped in (q.v.); (2) any solid surface which bears an image for printing.

point: the basic unit of type measurement in the English-speaking countries, approximately 1/72 inch.

portrait: a book or part of a book (e.g. an illustration or a table) which has a height greater than its width. See also *landscape.*

proof: except for a blockmaker's proof (q.v.), a roughly printed copy of text and/or illustrative matter for checking and correction. Not an indication of final printed quality. See *galley proof* and *page proof.*

quarto: (1) size of page when a sheet of paper is folded twice to make four leaves or eight pages, hence a book of this size; (2) a stationery size (10 × 8 inches).

quotes: inverted commas; quotation marks.

range left: set type with beginnings of lines aligned with left-hand margin.

range right: set type with ends of lines aligned with right-hand margin.

recto: right-hand page; *start recto* means start on right-hand page.

register: the accurate printing of an impression on a sheet in relation to other impressions already on the sheet; most frequently used with reference to the superimposition of one colour on another. *Out of register* means that two or more impressions are not correctly aligned.

repro pull: a high-quality proof printed on good paper and intended for photographic reproduction.

retouching: painting, spraying, or scratching photographs, transparencies, or artwork, in order to remove unwanted marks or alter parts of the picture before reproduction.

revise: a revised proof. A second stage of proofing after some corrections have been made.

river: an undesirable space running down several lines of type, caused by wide word-spacing and common in narrow, justified (q.v.) setting.

roman: ordinary upright type, as opposed to *italic*, which slants.

rule: (1) metal strip of type height which prints a line; (2) any printed straight line.

running head: a headline placed at the top of every ordinary text page, stating the title and/or the author of the work or the title of the chapter or section to which that page belongs.

run on: (1) continue on the same line without paragraph or other break; (2) print a further quantity of sheets, additional to the original order without stopping the printing machine.

sans serif: type face without serifs (q.v.). This is sans serif.

screen: dot pattern in halftone image (q.v.).

section: (1) signature (q.v.); (2) part of chapter or article.

serif: a small stroke at the top or bottom of a main stroke of a letter. See also *sans serif*.

set: (1) to assemble type by hand; (2) to key and cast type by machine; (3) the width of the body (q.v.) of a type character; the *set* of a fount is the width, in points, of the widest character.

set full out: set to the full type measure; do not indent.

set-off: the accidental transfer of ink from one printed sheet to another.

signature: a folded sheet, or part of a sheet, ready for sewing or perfect binding (q.v.). A signature usually comprises 16 or 32 pages but may be any multiple of 4 up to 64 pages. Also referred to as a *section* or *gathering*.

solid: without added leading between lines of type. Five lines of 10-point type *set solid* occupy a depth of 50 points.

solidus: oblique stroke /.

sort: a character of type. A *special sort* is a character which is not included in the standard fount (q.v.).

strike-on composition: method of setting by means of a sophisticated typewriter which produces camera copy (q.v.) of justified or unjustified (q.v.) type in a limited range of type faces. Also called *cold composition* or, when an IBM machine is used, *IBM setting*.

style: rules of an editorial or typographical nature adopted by a printer or publisher to ensure uniformity.

subscript: a small character or symbol which is printed below the base line of a full-size character. Preferably used to describe diacritical marks (q.v.) centred below the character. See *inferior*.

superior: a small numeral or other character which is printed above the x height (q.v.) of the normal characters in the text (e.g. a footnote reference number).

superscript: a small character or symbol which is printed above a full-size character (e.g. an accent or diacritical mark).

tip-in: a separately printed leaf pasted (*tipped*) into a book. Plates, foldouts, and errata slips are often *tipped in*.

type face: (1) the printing surface of a piece of type; (2) a particular type design.

type sizes: measured and denoted by the point system. Common sizes for text use are 8-point, 10-point, 11-point, and 12-point. The point measurement used in the English-speaking countries differs from that used in many other countries. Before about 1880 type sizes were arbitrary and were distinguished by names such as 'nonpareil' and 'bourgeois'.

unjustified: unjustified type has even word spacing, and if, as is usual, it is ranged left, it has a ragged right-hand margin.

verso: left-hand page; the opposite side of a leaf from the recto.

widow: the short last line of a paragraph when it appears at the top of a page. This is considered undesirable and may be avoided by altering the word spacing to shorten or lengthen the paragraph by one line, a time-consuming operation.

wrong fount: the accidental appearance in a piece of type-setting of a character which is of the wrong size or type face.

x height: a vertical dimension equal to the height of the lower-case letter x, which is the standard height of the lower-case alphabet not including the ascending and descending strokes. The measurement is used to define the size of the printed face, in relation to the body size, of a type face (see *body* above).

13
Useful Works of Reference

British Standards Institution, *BS 5261: Guide to Copy Preparation and Proof Correction, Part 1: Recommendations for Preparation of Typescript Copy for Printing* (London, 1975)

British Standards Institution, *BS 3700: The Preparation of Indexes for Books, Periodicals, and Other Publications* (London, 1964)

Butcher, Judith, *Copy-Editing: The Cambridge Handbook* (Cambridge, 1975)

Hart, Horace, *Hart's Rules for Compositors and Readers at the University Press, Oxford*, thirty-eighth edition (Oxford 1978)

Oxford University Press, *The Oxford Dictionary for Writers and Editors* (Oxford 1981)

University of Chicago Press, *A Manual of Style*, twelfth edition (Chicago, 1970)

14

Proof Correction

All corrections should be distinctly made in ink in the margins; marks made in the text should be those indicating the place to which the correction refers. An alteration is made by striking through, or marking as indicated in the table below, the character, word, or words to be altered, and writing the new material in the margin, followed by a concluding stroke (/). If several corrections occur in one line they should be divided between the left and right margins, the order being from left to right in each margin; individual marks should be separated by a concluding stroke. When words are changed, deleted, or added it is desirable on a galley proof and essential on a page proof to make changes on adjacent lines to compensate for the space occupied by the characters deleted or added. Otherwise a whole paragraph may have to be reset or pages of type altered as far as the end of the article or chapter.

When checking page proofs it is necessary to ensure not only that each correction marked on the galley proofs has been made, but also that no further errors have been introduced during the process of correction. Running headings and page-numbers should be carefully checked on page proofs. It is possible for a line of type at the head or foot of a page to be omitted when page proofs are made up from galleys; therefore these also should be carefully checked. It is often safer to check these points as a separate operation after reading through the page proofs in the normal way.

Normally only matter to be substituted for or added to the existing text should be written on the proof. If, however, there are any problems or comments to be brought to the attention of the printer, they should be written on the proof, encircled, and preceded by the word 'PRINTER' (in capitals).

The following table of proof correction marks is based on the *Guide to Copy Preparation and Proof Correction, Part 2* (BS 5261: Part 2: 1976) and material from this publication is reproduced by permission of the British Standards Institution, 2 Park Street, London W1A 2BS, from whom complete copies may be obtained.

E

Group A   General

Number	Instruction	Textual mark	Marginal mark	Notes
A1	Correction is concluded	None	/	Make after each correction
A2	Leave unchanged	– – – – – under characters to remain	✓ (circled)	
A3	Remove extraneous marks	Encircle marks to be removed	✗	e.g. film or paper edges visible between lines on bromide or diazo proofs
A3.1	Push down spacing material which has risen and printed between words or lines	Encircle blemish	⊥	
A4	Refer to appropriate authority anything of doubtful accuracy	Encircle word(s) affected	(?) circled	

Group B   Deletion, insertion and substitution

B1	Insert in text the matter indicated in the margin	⋏	New matter followed by ⋏	Indentical to B2
B2	Insert additional matter identified by a letter in a diamond	⋏	⋏ Followed by for example ⟨A⟩	The additional copy should be supplied with the corresponding letter marked on it in a diamond e.g. ⟨A⟩
B3	Delete	/ through character(s) or ⊢— through words to be deleted	♂	
B4	Delete and close up	⌒/ through character or ⊢—⊣ through characters e.g. chara̷cter charae̲cter	♂	

Number	Instruction	Textual mark	Marginal mark	Notes
B5	Substitute character or substitute part of one or more word(s)	/ through character or ⊢———⊣ through word(s)	New character or new word(s)	
B6	Wrong fount. Replace by character(s) of correct fount	Encircle character(s) to be changed	⊗	
B6.1	Change damaged character(s)	Encircle character(s) to be changed	✕	This mark is identical to A3
B7	Set in or change to italic	——— under character(s) to be set or changed	⊔⊔	Where space does not permit textual marks encircle the affected area instead
B8	Set in or change to capital letters	═══ under character(s) to be set or changed	≡	
B9	Set in or change to small capital letters	═══ under character(s) to be set or changed	═	
B9.1	Set in or change to capital letters for initial letters and small capital letters for the rest of the words	≡ under initial letters and ═══ under rest of the word(s)	≡	
B10	Set in or change to bold type	∿∿∿∿ under character(s) to be set or changed	∿	
B11	Set in or change to bold italic type	∿∿∿∿ under character(s) to be set or changed	⊔⊔∿∿	
B12	Change capital letters to lower case letters	Encircle character(s) to be changed	≢	For use when B5 is inappropriate

Number	Instruction	Textual mark	Marginal mark	Notes
B12.1	Change small capital letters to lower case letters	Encircle character(s) to be changed	≠	For use when B5 is inappropriate
B13	Change italic to upright type	Encircle character(s) to be changed	⊔	
B14	Invert type	Encircle character to be inverted	↻	
B15	Substitute or insert character in 'superior' position	/ through character or ⋏ where required	⌐ under character e.g. ⌐2	
B16	Substitute or insert character in 'inferior' position	/ through character or ⋏ where required	⌐ over character e.g. ⌐2	
B17	Substitute ligature e.g. ffi for separate letters	⊢———⊣ through characters affected	⌣ e.g. ffi	
B17.1	Substitute separate letters for ligature	⊢———⊣	Write out separate letters	
B18	Substitute or insert full stop or decimal point	/ through character or ⋏ where required	⊙	
B18.1	Substitute or insert colon	/ through character or ⋏ where required	⊙⊙	
B18.2	Substitute or insert semi-colon	/ through character or ⋏ where required	؛	

Number	Instruction	Textual mark	Marginal mark	Notes
B18.3	Substitute or insert comma	/ through character or ∧ where required	?	
B18.4	Substitute or insert apostrophe	/ through character or ∧ where required	'	
B18.5	Substitute or insert single quotation marks	/ through character or ∧ where required	' and/or '	
B18.6	Substitute or insert double quotation marks	/ through character or ∧ where required	" and/or "	
B19	Substitute or insert ellipsis	/ through character or ∧ where required	...	
B20	Substitute or insert leader dots	/ through character or ∧ where required	⊙	Give the measure of the leader when necessary
B21	Substitute or insert hyphen	/ through character or ∧ where required	⊢–⊣	
B22	Substitute or insert rule	/ through character ∧ where required	⊢—⊣	Give the size of the rule in the marginal mark e.g. ⊢1 em⊣ ⊢4 mm⊣

Number	Instruction	Textual mark	Marginal mark	Notes
B23	Substitute or insert oblique	/ through character or λ where required		

Group C Positioning and spacing

Number	Instruction	Textual mark	Marginal mark	Notes
C1	Start new paragraph			
C2	Run on (no new paragraph)			
C3	Transpose characters or words	between characters or words, numbered when necessary		
C4	Transpose a number of characters or words	3 2 1	1 2 3	To be used when the sequence cannot be clearly indicated by the use of C3. The vertical strokes are made through the characters or words to be transposed and numbered in the correct sequence
C5	Transpose lines			
C6	Transpose a number of lines		3 2 1	To be used when the sequence cannot be clearly indicated by C5. Rules extend from the margin into the text with each line to be transplanted numbered in the correct sequence
C7.	Centre	enclosing matter to be centred	[ ]	
C8	Indent			Give the amount of the indent in the marginal mark

Number	Instruction	Textual mark	Marginal mark	Notes
C9	Cancel indent			
C10	Set line justified to specified measure	and/or		Give the exact dimensions when necessary
C11	Set column justified to specified measure			Give the exact dimensions when necessary
C12	Move matter specified distance to the right	enclosing matter to be moved to the right		Give the exact dimensions when necessary
C13	Move matter specified distance to the left	enclosing matter to be moved to the left		Give the exact dimensions when necessary
C14	Take over character(s), word(s) or line to next line, column or page			The textual mark surrounds the matter to be taken over and extends into the margin
C15	Take back character(s), word(s), or line to previous line, column or page			The textual mark surrounds the matter to be taken back and extends into the margin
C16	Raise matter	over matter to be raised / under matter to be raised		Give the exact dimensions when necessary. (Use C28 for insertion of space between lines or paragraphs in text)
C17	Lower matter	over matter to be lowered / under matter to be lowered		Give the exact dimensions when necessary. (Use C29 for reduction of space between lines or paragraphs in text)
C18	Move matter to position indicated	Enclose matter to be moved and indicate new position		Give the exact dimensions when necessary

Number	Instruction	Textual mark	Marginal mark	Notes
C19	Correct vertical alignment			
C20	Correct horizontal alignment	Single line above and below misaligned matter e.g. miₛaligned		The marginal mark is placed level with the head and foot of the relevant line
C21	Close up. Delete space between characters or words	linking ⌢⌣ characters		
C22	Insert space between characters	| between characters affected		Give the size of the space to be inserted when necessary
C23	Insert space between words			Give the size of the space to be inserted when necessary
		between words affected		
C24	Reduce space between characters	| between characters affected		Give the amount by which the space is to be reduced when necessary
C25	Reduce space between words	between words affected		Give amount by which the space is to be reduced when necessary
C26	Make space appear equal between characters or words	| between characters or words affected		
C27	Close up to normal interline spacing	(each side of column linking lines)		The textual marks extend into the margin

Number	Instruction	Textual mark	Marginal mark	Notes
C28	Insert space between lines or paragraphs		or	The marginal mark extends between the lines of text. Give the size of the space to be inserted when necessary
C29	Reduce space between lines or paragraphs		or	The marginal mark extends between the lines of text. Give the amount by which the space is to be reduced when necessary

MARKS TO BE MADE ON PROOF, OR PROOFS, AFTER READING

Mark	Meaning
'Revise' (and signature)	Correct and submit another proof.
'Revise and make-up' (and signature)	Correct and submit another proof in page form.
'Revise and press' (and signature)	Make final corrections and print off without submitting another proof.
'Press' (and signature)	No correction necessary. The work may be printed.

PROOF CORRECTION

Marked galley proof of text

(B9.1) =/

At the sign of the red pale Y/

(B13) ⍴/

The Life and Work of William Caxton, by H W Larken

(C7) [ ]/

[An Extract] ↜/

(C9) ⅂/

Few people, even in the field of printing, have any clear =/
conception of what William Caxton did or, indeed, of
what he was. Much of this lack of knowledge is due to the
absence of information that can be counted as factual
and the consequent tendency to vague generalisation. i/

(B12) ≢/

Though it is well known that Caxton was born in the
county of Kent, there is no information as to the precise

(B18.5) ⸜/

place. In his prologue to the History of Troy, William Caxton
wrote 'for in France I was never and was born and ⟋/
learned my English in Kent in the Weald where I doubt

(B18.5) ⸍/

not is spoken as broad and rude English as in any place Y/
of England.' During the fifteenth century there were a ⌐/

(B6) Ⓚ/

great number of Flemish cloth weavers in Kent; most
of them had come to England at the instigation of
Edward III with the object of teaching their craft to the
English. So successful was this venture that the English t/

(B17) ﬁ/

cloth trade flourished and the agents who sold the cloth
(the mercers) became very wealthy people. There have b ♪/

(C8) ⌐/

There have been many speculations concerning the origin
of the Caxton family and much research has been carried
out. It is assumed often that Caxton's family must have ⌐/

(B14) Ω/

been connected with the wool trade in order to have
secured his apprenticeship to an influential merchant.

(A4) (?)/

W. Blyth Crotch (Prologues and Epilogues of William Ш/

(B7) Ш/

Caxton) suggests that the origin of the name Caxton (of
which there are several variations in spelling) may be
traced to Cambridgeshire but notes that many writers
have suggested that Caxton was connected with a family

(A3.1) ⊥/

at Hadlow or alternatively a family in Canterbury.

(B18.1) ⊙/

Of the Canterbury connection, a William Caxton =/
became freeman of the City in 1431 and William Pratt,

(B15) ⸜/

a mercer who was the printer's friend, was born there.
H. R. Plomer suggests that Pratt and Caxton might possibly
have been schoolboys together, perhaps at the school St.
Alphege. In this parish there lived a John Caxton who ⟨A⟩/

(C26) Ж/

used as his mark three cakes over a barrel (or tun) and
who is mentioned in an inscription on a monument in
the church of St. Alphege.

(Continued overleaf)

In 1941, Alan Keen (an authority on manuscripts)
secured some documents concerning Caxton; these are
now in the BRITISH MUSEUM. Discovered in the library of
Earl Winterton at Shillinglee Park by Richard Holworthy,
the documents cover the period 1420 to 1467. One of
Winterton's ancestors purchased the manor of West
Wratting from a family named Caxton, the property
being situated in the Weald of Kent.
There is also record of a property mentioning Philip
Caxton and his wife Dennis who had two sons, Philip
(born in 1413) and William.
Particularly interesting in these documents is one
recording that Philip Caxton junior sold the manor of
Little Wratting to John Christemasse of London in 1436,
the deed having been witnessed by two aldermen, one of
whom was Robert Large, the printer's employer.
Further, in 1439, the other son, William Caxton, con-
Wratting to John Christemasse, and an indenture of 1457
concerning this property mentions one William Caxton
veyed his rights in the manor Bluntes Hall at Little
alias Causton. It is an interesting coincidence to note that
the lord of the manor of Little Wratting was the father of
Margaret, Duchess of Burgundy.
In 1420, a Thomas Caxton of Tenterden witnessed the
will of a fellow townsman; he owned property in Kent and
appears to have been a person of some importance.

[1] See 'William Caxton'.

 attached to Christchurch Monastery in the parish of

Margin marks (right):
X / (A3)
≠ / (B12.1)
⌐⌐⌐ / (C2)
∂ / (B4)
1e H / (B22)
(C14)
H / (B21)
—2
—3 / (C6)
—1
⌐ / (C25)
(+1pt (C28)
) —1pt (C29)

Margin marks (left):
≡ / (K)
⊙ /
, /
⌒ /
||| /

15
Index

This index does not cover entries in the glossary or examples of proof corrections given on pages 60–69 since these can readily be consulted without the aid of an index.

abbreviations, 11–12
  in bibliographies, 42
  for currencies, 23
  in footnotes and endnotes, 11
  list of, 7; (in theses), 45
  for manuscripts, 38
  omissions, 12
  in references, 32
  for repositories, 38
  of titles, 11
  use of full stop in, 12
accents, 3, 5, 8
  on capitals, 18
acknowledgements, 7
  in theses, 45
alterations
  on proofs, 59
  on typescript, 2–3
ampersand, 9
apostrophe, 10
appendices, 7
  in theses, 43, 46
arabic numerals, 2, 36
articles, references to
  in books, 35
  in journals, 36
  in newspapers, 37
author–date system of references, 40
author's
  corrections, 3
  name, 1, 33
  preface, 7

Bible, references to, 38
bibliographical details, 6
bibliography, 7, 42
  in theses, 46
binding of theses, 49
bold type face, 4
books,
  early printed, 9
  parts of, 6
  titles of, 17
book titles, capitalization in, 17–18

brackets (square), 14
  in quotations, 26–27
  in references, 34

capitals, 16–18
  accented, 18
  for headings in typescript, 1
  in hyphenated compounds, 18
  for literary movements and periods, 17
  for literary works, 17–18
  in quotations, 24–25
  as roman numerals, 2, 22
  in titles and dignities, 16
captions, 5
  in theses, 49
centuries, 21
chapter titles, inverted commas for, 20
checking of typescripts, 3
  of theses, 48
collections of manuscripts, references
    to, 38
colon, 13
comma, 13
comments, on typescript, 2–3
compounds, 9
contents list, 6
  in theses, 44
contractions, 9
copies, number of
  of theses, 49
  of typescript, 2
copyright, 27
  of illustrations, 6
  international symbol, 7
  of theses, 50
correction marks, 59–69
correction
  of proofs, 59–69
  in theses, 48
  in typescripts, 2–3
cross-references, 6, 42
  in theses, 48–49
cultural movements, capitalization of, 17
currency, 22–23

dashes, 13
dates, 21–22
declaration in theses, 45
dedication, 6
dignities, capitalization of, 16
dissertations,
    presentation of, 43–50
    references to, 37
ditto, 13
drawings, 5

editor, name of, in references, 33
editorial comments, 14
editor's instructions to printer, 3, 5, 30
ellipsis, 15
    in quotations, 27
em rules, 13
endnotes, 29–30
    abbreviations in, 11
    methods of limiting, 29
    numbering, 2, 30
    in theses, 45–46
    in typescript, 2
en rules, 13
epigraph, 6
essays, titles of, 20
exclamation marks, 15
    in quotations, 26

facsimile reprints, references to, 31
Festschriften, references to, 33
figures (line illustrations), 5–6
    in theses, 49
footnotes, 29–30
    abbreviations in, 11
    methods of limiting, 29
    numbering, 2, 30
    in theses, 45–46
    in typescript, 2
foreign book titles, capitalization in, 17–18
foreign words and quotations
    in English usage, 8
    place-names, 10, 34, 42
    quotations, 24
    in typescript, 3–4
    use of italics, 19–20
foreword, 7
frontispiece, 7
full stop
    after abbreviations, 12
    in ellipsis, 15
    in expressing currencies, 22–23
    with parentheses, 14
    in quotations, 24–25, 27
    in references, 33, 35, 36

galley proofs, correction of, 59–69

glossary, 7
    in theses, 43

half-title, 6
headings,
    punctuation in, 14
    in theses, 48
    in typescript, 1
hyphenated compounds in titles, 18
hyphens
    in spelling, 8-9
    in titles, 18
    in typescript, 4

illustrations, 5–6
    captions for, 5–6
    lettering on, 5
    list of, 6; (in theses), 44
    numbering, 5
    originals, 5
    packing, 6
    size and reduction, 5
    in theses, 49
imprint, 7
index, 7
    in theses, 46
initial capitals, 16–18
initial letters in abbreviations, 12
insertions in typescript, 2
interpolations (in quotations), 26
introduction, 7
    in theses, 43, 45
italics, 19–20
    for emphasis, 19
    for foreign words and quotations, 19
    for Latin words and abbreviations,
        19–20
    punctuation with, 14–15
    in references, 32–38
    for titles of literary works, 20
    type face, 4

journals, references to articles in, 31,
    36–37

Latin quotations, 19
latinate abbreviations, 32, 39
learned societies, in references, 36
legal cases, citation of, 20
ligatures, 3
line division in verse quotations, 24
literary movements and periods,
    capitalization of, 17
lower case, 4

manuscripts, references to, 38
maps, 6

margins
  in theses, 47
  on typescripts, 1
medieval German quotations, 19

newspaper articles, references to, 37
non-roman characters, 3–5
notes, 2, 29–30
  abbreviations in, 11
  methods of limiting, 29
  numbering, 2, 30
  in theses, 45–46
  in typescript, 2
numbering
  illustrations, 5
  notes, 30
  pages, 7
  typescript pages, 1
numbers, 21–22
nunnation mark (tilde), 9

omissions
  in abbreviations, 12
  ellipsis, 15
  in quotations, 27
order of parts of a book, 6–7
ordinals, 21
original drawings, 5
original text, additions to, 14

page, abbreviations of, 11–12
page proof, checking, 59
  corrections, 59–69
pagination of typescripts, 1;
  (for theses), 48
paper for typescripts, 1
  for theses, 47
paragraph, indenting in typescript, 1
parentheses, 14
  in references, 25, 33, 35, 36, 37
parts of book, 6–7
permission to consult and copy theses, 50
philosophical movements, 17
phonetic transcription, square brackets
  in, 14
photographs, 5
place-names, 10
  in references, 34
plates (illustrations), 5–6
plays, references to, 37–38
plurals, abbreviation of, 12
poems,
  quotations from, 24–28
  references to long, 37–38
possessive, the, 10
preface, 7
  in theses, 45

preferred spelling, 8
preliminary pages, 6–7
  in theses, 43–45
printer, comments for, 3
proof corrections, 2, 59–69
prose,
  abbreviations in, 11
  quotations, 24–28
punctuation, 13–15
  after abbreviations, 12
  ellipsis, 15
  footnote numbers, 30
  in headings, 1, 14
  with italics, 14–15
  with parentheses, 14
  in quotations, 24–27
  with reference numbers, 2

question mark, 26
quotation marks, 24–27
  in references, 34, 35, 36, 37
  in titles, 20
quotations, 24–28
  copyright, 27–28
  in foreign languages, 19, 24
  long, 25–27
  omissions within, 27
  short, 24–25

references, 29, 31–42
  abbreviations in, 11
  author–date system of, 40–41
  to articles (in books), 35; (in journals),
    36–37; (in newspapers), 37
  to the Bible, 38
  in bibliographies, 42
  to books, 32–35
  cross-, 6, 42; (in theses), 48–49
  later, 39
  to manuscripts, 38
  to plays and long poems, 37–38
  after quotations, 25–27
  to repositories, 38–39, 41
  to theses, 37
  in typescript, 7; (in theses), 45–46
  to unpublished documents, 41
reprints, references to, 31
roman numerals, 22
  lower case, 2, 7
  in references, 33, 38
  in subdivisions, 2
running headings, 6

small capitals, 4, 38
spacing
  in theses, 47
  in typescripts, 1

spelling, 8–10
  accents, 8
  compounds, 9
  hyphens, 8–9
  place-names, 10
  the possessive, 10
  preferred, 8
  in quotations, 9
square brackets, 14
  in quotations, 26–27
  in references, 34
'strike-on' composition, 4
subdivisions, 2
subheadings
  in theses, 48
  in typescript, 1
summary of thesis, 44
superior
  figures, 30
  letters, 9
synopsis of thesis, 44

tables, 6
  copyright for, 28
  punctuation in, 14
  in theses, 44
theses,
  preparation of, 43–50
  references to, 37

tilde, 9
title-page, 6
  of thesis, 43–44
titles and dignities, 16
titles,
  abbreviations, 11, 12, 40, 41
  capitalization, 16, 17–18
  hyphenated compounds in, 18
  in italics, 20
  in references, 31–42
transliteration, 3–4
type faces (printers'), 4
  for theses (typewriter), 47
typescript, preparation of, 1–6;
  (for theses), 47–49
typing, 1
  theses, 43–49

underlining, 4
unusual characters,
  accented, 3–5, 8, 18
  non-roman, 3–5

verse quotations, 24–28

word-breaks in foreign languages, 4

xerox copies, 2
  of theses, 49

NOTES